Comparative Education

With Special Reference to Elementary Education

C. Naseema
V.K. Jibin

SHIPRA

ISBN: 978-81-7541-690-1

First Published in India in 2013

Comparative Education: With Special Reference to Elementary Education

Published by:
SHIPRA PUBLICATIONS
H.O.: LG 18-19, Pankaj Central Market, Patparganj,
Delhi-110092, Tel: 91-11-2223 5152, 2223 6152
Br.Off.: 4617/18, Ansari Road, Darya Ganj,
New Delhi-110002, Tel: 9650028065, 9810522367
E-mail: info@shiprapublications.com
www.shiprapublications.com

Preface

Education is the most important asset we have because our knowledge is the type of wealth that we can never lose, and the more we share it the more we are enlightened. However, basic knowledge starts with elementary education without which none of our dreams are possible. Elementary education is like the first step we take in life; we can never be able to run if we don't learn walking.

Education is a critical input in human resource development and is essential for the country's economic growth. Though the major indicators of socio-economic development viz., the growth rate of the economy, birth rate, death rate, infant mortality rate and literacy rate are all inter-connected, the literacy rate has been the major determinant of the rise or fall in comparison to the other indicators. There is enough evidence even in India to show that a high literacy rate, especially in the case of women, correlates with low birth rate, low infant mortality rate and increase in the rate of life expectancy. The recognition of this fact has created awareness on the need to focus upon literacy and elementary education programmes, not simply as a matter of social justice but more to foster economic growth, social well-being and social stability.

Today, education has been made available to all those who wish to study, there are centers available in every possible location and a vast number of online possibilities. Online resources are made available to those who are mentally and physically challenged as well as to those who cannot attend school due to any other reasons. Home schooling is an accredited form of studying encouraged by the government of the United States all over the country. Online home schooling offer qualified teachers and courses that are of the same standard to those who attend standard school daily.

The book is about the elementary education in different countries, as a comparison of nature of elementary education in India and some of the countries under different continents. The book aims to present overview of the systems adopted and different aspects of elementary education.

The first chapter of the book reflects a detailed discussion on national policy of education, important projects, Sarva Siksha Abhiyan(SSA), Rashtriya Madhyamik Shiksha Abhiyan (RMSA), Right to Education Act (RTE), Pre-school Education, Girls' Education, Special Schemes for girls and Children with special needs, Curriculum and Evaluation, Comprehensive and Continuous Evaluation, Teachers and teacher training, National Curriculum Framework in Indian context.

It also discusses problems of elementary education in developing countries. The chapter follows are giving a detailed description of elementary education in Asian countries, elementary education in Europe, elementary education in African countries, elementary education in Australia, elementary education in Latin America, and elementary education in North America.

The book is specially intended to the teachers training courses like D.Ed, T.T.C., B.Ed, M.Ed. and M.A (Education) level covered by different states . It will also contribute to the policy makers while framing curricula at school level. It is hoped that this book will be useful to the students, teachers, prospective teachers and teacher educators and all others who are concerned with elementary education.

C. Naseema
V.K. Jibin

CONTENTS

1
Elementary Education in India

INTRODUCTION

Education plays an integral part in the overall development of the personality. The government has come up with unique steps to make primary education compulsory for all. In simple words, elementary education implies eight years of compulsory schooling that begins from the age of six. The government ensures to make elementary education free and compulsory for all.

Since Independence, India has made impressive progress in terms of growth of educational institutions at different levels, physical access to schooling for children, and diversification of educational programmes. Today, 18 crore children are taught by almost 57 lakh teachers in more than 12 lakh primary and upper primary schools across the length and breadth of the country. With schematic interventions from the erstwhile Operation Blackboard, Bihar Education Project, Lok Jumbish, District Primary Education Programme, and the Government's current flagship programme of Sarva Shiksha Abhiyan (SSA), over 98 per cent of our children are estimated to have access to primary schooling within one kilometer of their habitation, and almost 92 per cent to an upper primary school within three kilometers of their habitation. Gross enrolment ratios have increased significantly across all social categories, drop out rates at primary level have declined, and transition from primary to upper primary stage has improved.

Decentralised academic support structures have been established in the form of District Institutes for Education and Training (DIETs) in 571 districts, and Resource Centres in 6746 blocks and 70388 clusters in the country. Over 12 crore children participate in the Mid Day Meal programme, the world's largest school feeding programme, which impacts not only enrollment of children, but also their regular attendance in school and participation in the learning process.

After the inception of DPEP (District Primary Education Programme) in 1994, the government came up with the SSA or "Sarva Shiksha Abhiyan" in 2001 so as to bring in an improvement in the elementary education system. Lowering the poverty ratio, promoting female literacy, and emphasizing on rural education will help SSP fulfill their desired goal. For optimum management control, the government has also joined hands with the School Management Committees, Tribal Autonomous Councils, Mother Teacher Associations as well as the Village and Urban Slum Level Education Committees. The SSA aims at improving the ratio of teaches to students, emphasize more on teachers training, provide learning materials for teachers and textbooks for children as well as make every possible effort for their academic support.

In addition, the government has also introduced compulsory elementary education, exclusively for girls. For instance, the Kasturba Gandhi Shiksha Yojana aims to come up with residential schools in districts (particularly the ones with low literacy rate amongst females) for girls. Institutes such as National Bal Bhavan helps students pursue their desired activities and improve their creative ability in the process. Besides, there are other programmes like Mid Day Meal Scheme to help allure an increasing number of children towards literacy.

At the time of adoption of the Constitution in 1950, the aim was to achieve the goal of Universalisation of Elementary Education (UEE) within the next ten years i.e. by 1960. Keeping in view the educational facilities available in the country at that time, the goal was far too ambitious to achieve within a short span of ten years. Hence, the target date was shifted a number of times. Till 1960, all efforts were focused on provision of schooling facilities. It was only after the near realization of the goal of access that other components of UEE, such as universal enrolment and retention, started receiving attention of planners and policy makers. It is the *Quality of Education*, which is at present in the focus in all programmes relating to elementary education in general and primary education in particular.

Significant efforts have been made in the last sixty years to universalize elementary education.

Since 1950, impressive progress has been made in every sphere of elementary education. In 1950-51, there were about 210 thousand primary and 14 thousand upper primary schools. Their numbers are now increased to 627 thousand and 190 thousand respectively as in the year 1998-99; thus showing an average annual growth of 2.30 and 5.58 per cent per annum. As many as 83 per cent of the total 1,061 thousand habitations have access to primary schooling facilities within 1 km and 76 per cent habitations to upper primary schooling facilities within a distance of 3 km. About 94 and 85 per cent of the total rural population is accessed to primary and upper primary schools/sections. More than 84 per cent of the total 570 thousand primary schools in 1993-94 had school buildings. The number of single-teacher primary schools has also considerably declined.

The number of teachers both at the primary and upper primary levels of education over time has increased many folds. From a low of 538 thousand in 1950-51, the number of primary school teachers in 1998-99 increased to 1,904 thousand (MHRD, 2000a). Similarly, upper primary teachers during the same period increased from 86 thousand to 1,278 thousand.

According to Arun C. Mehta, the analysis is confined to all-India level, however wherever necessary, state-specific situation is also analyzed. First the composition of school education across the states is presented. Some of the indicators that are developed and analyzed are literacy rates, habitations covered by schooling facilities, enrolment rates, attendance rates, transition rates, percentage of female teachers, average number of teachers in schools, trained teachers, facilities available in schools, pupil-teacher ratio, ratio of primary to upper primary schools and indicators of internal efficiency of education system. In addition, out-of-school children and additional enrolment that would be required to achieve the goal of universal enrolment is also worked-out. Further, Mehta observed the recent enrolment projection exercises and attempts to redefine the concept of universal elementary education. The government has initiated a number of programmes under the Centrally Sponsored Schemes to achieve the goal of EFA in general and UEE in particular;

Availability of schooling facilities is measured by a set of indicators concerning to access. As per norms, a habitation is entitled to have a primary school, if it has a total population of 300 and more and has no school within a distance of one kilometre. For upper primary schools, the corresponding norm is total population of 500 & more and a distance of three kilometres. However, the norm is often relaxed in case of hilly and tribal dominated areas, difficult terrains and border districts. A distance of one and three kilometre is treated as the maximum walking distance to which a child is expected to travel from his residence to school. The states have their own norms according to which they provide schooling facilities. Micro planning and school mapping related activities play an important role in making provision for schools and also deciding location where a school is to be opened. Efforts have been made in the recent past to conduct micro planning and school mapping exercises under the DPEP and Lok Jumbish Project.

Over a period of time, facilities in schools have improved significantly but still a large number of primary schools do not have adequate facilities that are required for smooth functioning of a school. Both the Central and State Governments had initiated a number of programmes to improve facilities, one such programme is the Operation Blackboard Scheme.

Of the total 0.57 million primary schools in 1993-94, only 65.01 per cent had *pucca* (permanent) buildings. The rest of the schools had either partially permanent buildings or were functioning in open space or even in tents (4.20 per cent, 24 thousand schools). Of the total building-less schools, government schools constitute more than 65 per cent, whereas schools managed by private organizations do not have any such school. On the other hand only a few upper primary schools in 1993-94 were functioning in open space/tents (2,966). Even if a school has building that need not guarantee that it has got adequate number of instructional rooms. Most of the primary schools on an average had 2 instructional rooms, which is less than the total number of grades/ sections a school has got. But there are several schools, which had more than even 10 rooms. On the other hand an upper primary school on an average had four rooms. Further, it has been noticed that the majority of primary schools did not have ancillary facilities in 1993-94. The drinking water facility was available in only 44.23 per cent primary schools against which 18.93 per cent had urinal facility in school. Further, it is noticed that government run schools had poor facilities than in schools managed by the private organizations.

Even if the schools have necessary infrastructure that itself is not a guarantee that it has also got adequate number of teachers of the total 0.57 million primary schools in 1993-94, only 65.01 per cent had *pucca* (permanent) buildings. The rest of the schools had either partially permanent buildings or were functioning in open space or even in tents. Of the total building-less schools, government schools constitute more than 65 per cent, whereas schools managed by private organizations do not have any such school. On the other hand only a few upper primary schools in 1993-94 were functioning in open space/tents. Even if a school has building that need not guarantee that it has got adequate number of instructional rooms. Most of the primary schools on an average had 2 instructional rooms, which is less than the total number of grades/sections a school has got. But there are several schools, which had more than even 10 rooms. On the other hand an upper primary school on an average had four rooms. Further, it has been noticed that the majority of primary schools did not have ancillary facilities in 1993-94. The drinking water facility was available in only 44.23 per cent primary schools against which 18.93 per cent had urinal facility in school. Further, it is noticed that government run schools had poor facilities than in schools managed by the private organizations. Even if the schools have necessary infrastructure that itself is not a guarantee that it has also got adequate number of teachers.

During 1990-98, primary and upper primary teachers increased respectively by 288 and 205 thousand. Despite the significant achievements still a large number of teachers' positions in a number of states are lying vacant mostly because of the court cases. Without diluting the academic qualifications states, such as, Gujarat, Rajasthan and Madhya Pradesh have appointed *para teachers.* The qualification requirement to become a primary or upper primary school teacher is generally 10 years of general education followed by one or two years of pre-service training. However, in the recent past many states have increased qualification requirements for elementary school teachers and pre-service training is also not a pre condition. Once the teachers are appointed, they are imparted in-service training duration of which vary from state to state.

Teachers are generally appointed for the elementary level and then they are deployed either in primary or upper primary school.

Considerable progress has been made so far as enrolment at primary and upper primary levels of education is concerned. Enrolment at the primary level was 19.16 million in 1950-51; which has now been increased to 110.9 million in 1998-99. Compared to primary level, the growth in enrolment at the upper primary level is much impressive and substantial but is not adequate to attain the status of universal enrolment.

Since independence, India has made considerable progress towards the goal of UEE. However, past trends do not indicate that the goal is right now in the sight. However, the trend can be reversed and goal may be achieved earlier than projected, if concerted efforts are made to bring all concerned under the umbrella of education. The Union Government initiated a number of projects and programmes under the *Centrally Sponsored Schemes* most of which have been initiated after the *National Policy of Education* was evolved in 1986 and *World Conference on Education for All* held at Jomtien in 1990. Some of these projects in terms of their objectives and major achievements are briefly discussed below:

NATIONAL POLICIES OF EDUCATION

The system of education introduced by the British Government in India was not suitable to needs of free, independent and developing India. Since our independence, India tried to restructure its education policy to suit the needs of technological and industrial developments.

Since the nation's independence in 1947, the Indian government sponsored a variety of programmes to address the problems of illiteracy in both rural and urban India. Maulana Abul Kalam Azad, India's first Minister of Education, envisaged strong central government control over education throughout the country, with a uniform educational system. The Union government established the University Education Commission (1948–1949) and the Secondary Education Commission (1952–1953) to develop proposals to modernise India's education system. The Resolution on Scientific Policy was adopted by the government of Jawaharlal Nehru, India's first Prime Minister. The Nehru government sponsored the development of high-quality scientific education institutions such as the Indian Institutes of Technology. In 1961, the Union government formed the National Council of Educational Research and Training (NCERT) as an autonomous organisation that would advise both the Union and state governments on formulating and implementing education policies.

Several Commissions under the chairmanship of well known educationists have been setup in the past.

In January 1985, immediately after the new government of Rajiv Gandhi came to power, it was announced that the Government would publish a document on education which would form the base for new education policy for the country. Accordingly "Challenge of Education—a policy perspective" was published by the Ministry of Education in August, 1985. After studying the views and suggestions received form various quarters, a new education policy was formulated in 1986 and it is known as 'National Policy on Education'.

The concept of a National System of Education implies that, up to a given level all students, irrespective of caste, creed, sex have access to education of a comparable quality. The common educational structure of 10+2+3 has been accepted. The system is based on a national circular framework, which contains a common core along with other component that are flexible. Common core shall be designed to promote democracy, socialism, equality of sexes, protection of environment, removal of social barriers, observance for small fairly norms and international co-operation and peaceful coexistence. Minimum levels of learning will be laid down for each stage of education. In the case of higher and technical education steps will be taken to facilitate interregional mobility by providing equal access to every Indian of requisite merit regardless of his place of birth.

The new policy laid special emphasis on the removal of disparities and to equalize educational opportunity by attending to the specific needs, of those who have been denied equality so far. In order to neutralize the accumulated distortion of the past, there will be a well-conceived edge in favor of women education which will be used as an agent of basic change in their status. Special measures are contemplated for education of Scheduled Castes, Scheduled Tribes, minorities and the children with special needs. Voluntary efforts for the education of the disabled is encouraged. A vast programme of adult and continuing education was also proposed to implement.

The new thrust in elementary education emphasized two aspects: (i) universal enrollment and universal retention of children upto 14 years of age, and (ii) a substantial improvement in the quality of education, provision was made for essential facilities in primary schools. A large and systematic programme of non-formal education was launched for school drop-outs, for children from villages and localities without schools, working boys and girls who cannot attend whole-day schools.

Secondary education begins to expose students to the differentiated role of science, humanities and social sciences. Conscious raising and a bent of healthy mind and imbibing human and cultural values were brought about through appropriately formulated curricula. The children with special talent or aptitude were provided opportunities to proceed at a faster pace. Pace-setting schools (called Navodya Vidhyalayas distinct from the Kandriya Vidhyalayas) were established in various parts of the country on a given pattern with full scope for innovation and experimentation. These school were became 'catalysts of a nationwide programme of school improvement.

Vocational education is a distinct stream. It would prepare students for identified occupations covering several areas of activity. These courses would normally be provided after the secondary stage, but keeping the scheme flexible, they may be made available after class VII also. In regard to higher education, stress had been laid on improvement of existing universities and institutions. According to Policy paper the main emphasis was on the consolidation and expansion of facilities in these institutions. The courses and programmes were proposed to be redesigned to meet the demands of specialization. Open university system was extended. Degrees were de-linked from jobs in selected areas.

Under the policies, system of planning and management of education was proposed to be overhauled on a high priority basis. For the purpose long term planning and management perspective of education was evolved. Educational institutions to be given autonomy and non-governmental agencies and voluntary effort is to be associated. At the national level Cultural Advisory Board of Education played a pivotal role in reviewing educational development. It is also proposed to establish an All India Education Service.

Commission 1968

Based on the report and recommendations of the Education Commission (1964–1966), the government of Prime Minister Indira Gandhi announced the first National Policy on Education in 1968, which called for a "radical restructuring" and equalise educational opportunities in order to achieve national integration and greater cultural and economic development. The policy called for fulfilling compulsory education for all children up to the age of 14, as stipulated by the Constitution of India, and the better training and qualification of teachers. The policy called for focus on learning of regional languages, outlining the "three language formula" to be implemented in secondary education—the instruction of the English language, the official language of the state where the school was based, and Hindi, the national language. Language education was seen as essential to reduce the gulf between the intelligentsia and the masses. Although the decision to adopt Hindi as the national language had proven controversial, the policy called for use and learning of Hindi to be encouraged uniformly to promote a common language for all Indians. The policy also encouraged the teaching of the ancient Sanskrit language, which was considered an essential part of India's culture and heritage. The NPE of 1968 called for education spending to increase to six percent of the national income.

Commission 1986

Having announced that a new policy was in development in January, 1985, the government of Prime Minister Rajiv Gandhi introduced a new National Policy on Education in May, 1986. The new policy called for "special emphasis on the removal of disparities and to equalise educational opportunity," especially for Indian women, Scheduled Tribes (ST) and the Scheduled Caste (SC) communities. To achieve these, the policy called for expanding scholarships, adult education, recruiting more teachers from the SCs, incentives for poor families to send their children to school regularly, development of new institutions and providing housing and services. The NPE called for a "child-centred approach" in primary education, and launched "Operation Blackboard" to improve primary schools nationwide. The policy expanded the open university system with the Indira Gandhi National Open University, which had been created in 1985. The policy also called for the creation of the "rural university" model, based on the philosophy of Indian leader Mahatma Gandhi, to promote economic and social development at the grassroots level in rural India robin.

Commission 1992

The 1986 National Policy on Education was modified in 1992 by the P.V. Narasimha Rao government. In 2005, Prime Minister Manmohan Singh adopted a new policy based on the "Common Minimum Programme" of his United Progressive Alliance (UPA) government. Programme of Action (PoA), 1992 under the National Policy on Education (NPE), 1986 envisaged conduct of a common entrance examination on all India basis for admission to professional and technical programmes in the country. For admission to Engineering and Architecture/Planning programmes, Government of India vide Resolution dated 18 October 2001 has laid down a Three-Exam Scheme (JEE and AIEEE at the National Level and the State Level Engineering Entrance Examinations (SLEEE) for State Level Institutions—with an option to join AIEEE). This takes care of varying admission standards in these programmes and helps in maintenance of professional standards. This also solves problems of overlaps and reduces physical, mental and financial burden on students and their parents due to multiplicity of entrance examinations.

IMPORTANT PROJECTS

Scheme of Operation Blackboard

The scheme of *Operation Blackboard* (OB) was launched in 1987 to improve facilities in schools by providing for more teachers, rooms and teaching learning equipments. The OB Scheme seeks to bring both the quantitative and qualitative improvements in primary education. The scheme had three components, namely (i) an additional teacher to single teacher primary schools; (ii) providing at least two classrooms in each primary school; and (iii) providing teaching-learning equipment to all primary schools. The scheme is implemented through the State Governments with 100 per cent assistance from the Central Government towards the salary of additional teachers and teaching learning equipments. It was proposed to cover all primary schools under the OB scheme that were in existence as on September 30, 1986.

National Programme for Nutritional Support (Mid-day Meal)

The *National Programme for Nutritional Support* to *Primary Education* (launched in 1995) provides food grains/cooked meals to children in primary classes. The programme assures 100 grams of grains per day for attending schools for at least 80 per cent of the total school days in a month. The programme had benefited more than 98 million children spread over 0.69 million schools. In the latest year, about 9.90 million children are covered under the scheme and allocated 2.71 million metric tones of grains (Annual Report: MHRD, 1999-2000). Along with teachers, local community is also given responsibility in the distribution of grains. In previous years, a significant gap has been noticed in quantity of food grains sanctioned and actually lifted

District Primary Education Project (DPEP)

The DPEP is a centrally sponsored scheme providing special thrust to achieve UEE. It takes a holistic view of primary education development and seeks to operationalise the strategy of UPE through district specific planning with emphasis on decentralized management, participatory processes, empowerment and capacity building at all levels. DPEP aims at providing access to primary education for all children, reducing primary dropout rate to less than 10 per cent, increasing learning achievement of primary school students by at least 25 per cent, and reducing the gap among gender and social groups to less than five per cent

Lok Jumbish and Shiksha Karmi Projects (LJP and SKP)

Apart from DPEP, *Lok Jumbish* (Peoples' Movement) and *Shiksha*

Karmi Projects are the other two important programmes, which are, received attention at the international level. Both these projects are under implementation in Rajasthan since 1992, which is one of the most educationally backward states of India. Lok Jumbish and Shiksha Karmi are funded by SIDA. The main objective of LJP is to achieve EFA through people's mobilization and participation. Whereas, SKP focuses it attention on universalisation and qualitative improvement of primary education in remote, arid area and socio-economically backward villages with primary attention given to girls. The project identifies teacher absenteeism as a major obstacle in achieving the goal of UEE

However, it may be noted that the LJP has covered only 75 blocks, which is just one quarter of the total blocks in Rajasthan. The management cost of LJP is high compared to other programmes of similar nature. It is also not known whether the success it has achieved, will it able to replicate elsewhere in Rajasthan and outside Rajasthan. The school mapping exercises, which are conducted under the LJP, though termed as school mapping but in fact, is a micro planning exercise.

Sarva Shiksha Abhiyan (SSA)

In addition to the Centrally Sponsored Schemes, states have initiated schemes to give momentum to their efforts towards the goal *of Education for All*. Later, the Government of India has also initiated an ambitious programme called *Sarva Shiksha Abhiyan* (SSA): *An Initiative for Universal Elementary Education* to achieve the goal of UEE. The programme is initially planned to initiate in about 50 low female districts spread over fifteen states. Unlike the *District Primary Education Programme*, the SSA envisages to develop district-specific elementary education plans within the framework of decentralized management of education with a focus on *Panchayati Raj Institutions*. A detailed overview of SSA is presented below.

SARVA SHIKSHA ABHIYAN—MOVEMENT OF EDUCATION FOR ALL

Sarva Shiksha Abhiyan has been implemented across India to achieve the long-cherished goal of Universalization of Elementary

Education through a time-bound integrated approach, in partnership with the States. Sarva Shiksha Abhiyan, which promises to change the pace of the elementary education sector in the country, aims to provide useful and quality elementary education to all children in the 6-14 age groups by 2010. The Sarva Shiksha Abhiyan is an effort to recognize the need for improving the performance of the school system and to provide community owned quality elementary education in mission mode. It also envisages bridging of gender and social gaps. The major objectives of SSA were the following:

- All children in schools, Education Guarantee Centre, Alternative School, 'Back-to-School' camp by 2003.
- All children complete five years of primary schooling by 2007.
- All children complete eight years of elementary schooling by 2010.
- Focus on elementary education of satisfactory quality with emphasis on education for life.
- Bridge all gender and social category gaps at primary stage by 2007 and at elementary education level by 2010.
- Universal retention by 2010.

The Sarva Shiksha Abhiyan was to provide useful and relevant elementary education for all children in the 6 to 14 age group by 2010. But still after 2010, it is continuing. Another goal is to bridge social, regional and general gaps, with the active participation of the community.

Useful and relevant education signifies a quest for an education system that is not alienating and that draws on community solidarity. Its aim is to allow children to learn about and master their natural environment in a manner that allows the fullest harnessing of their human potential. This quest must also be a process of value based learning that allows children an opportunity to work for each other's well being rather than to permit mere selfish pursuits.

SSA implemented the Pre-Project Activities and as a part of which it carried out the household survey. Based on the household survey all districts have formulated a Perspective Plan for 10 year period 2001-2010. SSA is being implemented in partnership with State Governments to cover the entire country and address the needs of 200 million children in nearly 2 million habitations. The programme seeks to open new schools in those habitations which do not have schooling facilities and strengthen existing school infrastructure through provision of additional class-rooms, toilets, drinking water, maintenance grant and school improvement grant. SSA has a special focus on girl's education and children with special needs.

Basic Features of Sarva Shiksha Abhiyan

Sarva Shiksha Abhiyan was an effort to universalise elementary education by community-ownership of the school system. It is a response to the demand for quality basic education all over the country. The SSA programme was also an attempt to provide an opportunity for improving human capabilities to all children, through provision of community-owned quality education in a mission mode. Sarva Shiksha Abhyan has the following features:

The Sarva Shiksha Abhiyan was to provide useful and relevant elementary education for all children in the 6 to 14 age group by 2010. There was also another goal to bridge social, regional and gender gaps, with the active participation of the community in the management of schools.

Useful and relevant education signifies a quest for an education system that is not alienating and that draws on community solidarity. Its aim is to allow children to learn about and master their natural environment in a manner that allows the fullest harnessing of their human potential both spiritually and materially. This quest must also be a process of value based learning that allows children an opportunity to work for each other's well being rather than to permit mere selfish pursuits.

Framework for Implementation (and Not a Guideline)

For the SSA a frame work for implementation in formed due to the following reasons:

- To allow states to formulate context specific guidelines within the overall framework
- To encourage districts in States and UTs to reflect local specificity
- To promote local need based planning based on broad National Policy norms
- To make planning a realistic exercise by adopting broad national norms.

The objectives are expressed nationally though it is expected that various districts and States are likely to achieve universalisation in their own respective contexts and in their own time frame. 2010 is the outer limit for such achievements. The emphasis is on mainstreaming out-of-school children through diverse strategies, as far as possible, and on providing eight years of schooling for all children in 6-14 age group. The thrust is on bridging of gender and social gaps and a total retention of all children in schools. Within this framework it is expected that the education system will be made relevant so that children and parents find the schooling system useful and absorbing, according to their natural and social environment.

SARVA SHIKSHA ABHIYAN AS A FRAMEWORK AND AS A PROGRAMME

Sarva Shiksha Abhiyan (SSA) has two aspects—1. It provides a wide convergent framework for implementation of Elementary Education schemes; 2. It is also a programme with budget provision for strengthening vital areas to achieve universalisation of elementary education. While all investments in the elementary education sector from the State and the Central Plans will reflect as part of the SSA framework, they will all merge into the SSA programme within the next few years. As a programme, it reflects the additional resource provision for UEE.

Broad Strategies Central to SSA Programme

- *Institutional Reforms*—As part of the SSA, the central and the State governments will undertake reforms in order to improve efficiency of the delivery system. The states will have to make an objective assessment of their prevalent education system including educational administration, achievement levels in schools, financial issues, decentralisation and community ownership, review of State Education Act, rationalization of teacher deployment and recruitment of teachers, monitoring and evaluation, status of education of girls, SC/ST and disadvantaged groups, policy regarding private schools and ECCE. Many States have already carried out several changes to improve the delivery system for elementary education.

- *Sustainable Financing*—The Sarva Shiksha Abhiyan is based on the premise that financing of elementary education interventions has to be sustainable. This calls for a long -term perspective on financial partnership between the Central and the State governments.
- *Community Ownership*—The programme calls for community ownership of school-based interventions through effective decentralisation. This will be augmented by involvement of women's groups, VEC members and members of Panchayati Raj institutions.
- *Institutional Capacity Building*—The SSA conceives a major capacity building role for national, state and district level institutions like NIEPA/NCERT/NCTE/SCERT/ SIEMAT/DIET.
- *Improvement in quality* requires a sustainable support system of resource persons and institutions.
- *Improving Mainstream Educational Administration*—It calls for improvement of mainstream educational administration by institutional development, infusion of new approaches and by adoption of cost effective and efficient methods.
- *Community Based Monitoring with Full Transparency*—The Programme will have a community based monitoring system. The Educational Management Information System (EMIS) will correlate school level data with community-based information from micro planning and surveys. Besides this, every school will be encouraged to share all information with the community, including grants received. A notice board would be put up in every school for this purpose.

- ***Habitation as a Unit of Planning***—The SSA works on a community based approach to planning with habitation as a unit of planning. Habitation plans will be the basis for formulating district plans.
- ***Accountability to Community***—SSA envisages cooperation between teachers, parents and PRIs, as well as accountability and transparency to the community.
- ***Priority to Education of Girls***—Education of girls, especially those belonging to the scheduled castes and scheduled tribes and minorities, will be one of the principal concerns in Sarva Shiksha Abhiyan.
- ***Focus on Special Groups***—There will be a focus on the inclusion and participation of children from SC/ST, minority groups, urban deprived children disadvantaged groups and the children with special needs, in the educational process.
- ***Pre-Project Phase***—SSA will commence throughout the country with a well-planned pre-project phase that provides for a large number of interventions for capacity development to improve the delivery and monitoring system. These include provision for household surveys, community-based microplanning and school mapping, training of community leaders, school level activities, support for setting up information system, office equipment, diagnostic studies, etc.,
- ***Thrust on Quality***—SSA lays a special thrust on making education at the elementary level useful and relevant for children by improving the curriculum, child-centered activities and effective teaching learning strategies.
- ***Role of Teachers***—SSA recognizes the critical and central role of teachers and advocates a focus on their development needs. Setting up of Block Resource Centres/ Cluster Resource Centres, recruitment of qualified teachers, opportunities for teacher development through participation in curriculum-related material development, focus on classroom process and exposure visits for teachers are all designed to develop the human resource among teachers.
- ***District Elementary Education Plans***—As per the SSA framework, each district will prepare a District Elementary

Education Plan reflecting all the investments being made and required in the elementary education sector, with a holistic and convergent approach. There will be a Perspective Plan that will give a framework of activities over a longer time frame to achieve UEE. There will also be an Annual Work Plan and Budget that will list the prioritized activities to be carried out in that year. The Perspective Plan will also be a dynamic document subject to constant improvement in the course of Programme Implementation.

Norms for Interventions under SSA

	Intervention	*Norm*
1.	Teacher	▪ One teacher for every 40 children in Primary and upper primary ▪ At least two teachers in a Primary school ▪ One teacher for every class in the upper primary
2.	School / Alternative schooling facility	• Within one Kilometre of every habitation • Provision for opening of new schools as per State norms or for setting up EGS like schools in unserved habitations.
3.	Upper Primary schools/ Sector	• As per requirement based on the number of children completing primary education, up to a ceiling of one upper primary school/section for every two primary schools
4.	Classrooms	• A room for every teacher in Primary & upper Primary, with the provision that there would be two class rooms with verandah to every Primary school with at least two teachers. • A room for Head-Master in upper Primary school/section
5.	Free textbooks	• To all girls/SC/ST children at primary & upper primary level within an upper ceiling of Rs. 150/- per child • State to continue to fund free textbooks • being currently provided from the State Plans.
6.	Civil works	• Ceiling of 33% of SSA programme funds. • For improvement of school facilities, BRC/CRC construction.

(*Contd.*)

(*Contd.*)

	Intervention	Norm
		• CRCs could also be used as an additional room. • No expenditure to be incurred on construction of office buildings • Districts to prepare infrastructure Plans.
7.	Maintenance and repair of school buildings	• Only through school management committees/VECs • Upto Rs. 5000 per year as per specific proposal by the school committee. • Must involve elements of community contribution
8.	Upgradation of EGS to regular school or setting up of a new Primary school as per State norm	• Provision for TLE @ Rs 10,000/- per school • TLE as per local context and need • Involvement of teachers and parents necessary in TLE selection and procurement • VEC/ school-village level appropriate body to decide on best mode of procurement • Requirement of successful running of EGS centre for two years before it is considered for upgradation. • Provision for teacher & classrooms.
9.	TLE for upper-primary	• @ Rs 50,000 per school for uncovered schools. • As per local specific requirement to be determined by the teachers/ school committee • School committee to decide on best mode of procurement, in consultation with teachers • School Committee may recommend district level procurement if there are advantages of scale.
10.	Schools grant	• Rs. 2000/- per year per primary/upper primary school for replacement of non functional school equipment • Transparency in utilisation • To be spent only by VEC/SMC
11.	Teacher grant	• Rs 500 per teacher per year in primary and upper primary • Transparency in utilisation
12.	Teacher training	• Provision of 20 days In-service course for all teachers each year, 60 days refresher course for untrained teachers already employed as teachers, and 30 days orientation for freshly trained recruits @ Rs. 70/- per day

(*Contd.*)

(*Contd.*)

	Intervention	Norm
		• Unit cost is indicative; would be lower in non residential training programmes • Includes all training cost • Assessment of capacities for effective training during appraisal will determine extent of coverage. • Support for SCERT/DIET under existing Teacher Education Scheme
13.	State Institute of Educational Management and Training (SIEMAT)	• One time assistance up to Rs. 3 crore • States have to agree to sustain • Selection criteria for faculty to be rigorous
14.	Training of community leaders	• For a maximum of 8 persons in a village for 2 days in a year - preferably women • @ Rs. 30/- per day
15.	Provision for disabled children	• Upto Rs. 1200/- per child for integration of disabled children, as per specific proposal, per year • District Plan for children with special needs will be formulated within the Rs. 1200 per child norm • Involvement of resource institutions to be encouraged
16.	Research, Evaluation, supervision and monitoring	• Up to Rs. 1500 per school per year • Partnership with research and resource institutions, pool of resource teams with State specific focus • Priority to development of capacities for appraisal and supervision through resource/ research institutions and on an effective EMIS • Provision for regular school mapping/micro planning for up dating of household data • By creating pool of resource persons, providing travel grant and honorarium for monitoring, generation of community-based data, research studies, cost of assessment and appraisal terms & their field activities, classroom observation by resource persons • Funds to be spent at national, state, district, sub district, school level out of the overall per school allocation. • Rs. 100 per school per year to be spent at national level

(*Contd.*)

(Contd.)

	Intervention	Norm
		• Expenditure at State/district/BRC/CRC/ School level to be decided by State/UT, This would include expenditure on appraisal, supervision, MIS, classroom observation, etc. Support to SCERT over and above the provision under the Teacher Education scheme may also be provided. • Involvement of resource institutions willing to undertake state specific responsibilities
17.	Management Cost	• Not to exceed 6% of the budget of a district plan • To include expenditure on office expenses, hiring of experts at various levels after assessment of existing manpower, POL, etc.; • Priority to experts in MIS, community planning processes, civil works, gender, etc. depending on capacity available in a particular district • Management costs should be used to develop effective teams at State/ District/ Block/ Cluster levels • Identification of personnel for BRC/ CRC should be a priority in the pre-project phase itself so that a team is available for the intensive process based planning.
18.	Innovative activity for girls' education, early childhood care & education, interventions for children belonging to SC/ ST community, computer education specially for upper primary level	• Upto to Rs. 15 lakh for each innovative project and Rs. 50 lakh for a district per year will apply for SSA • ECCE and girls education interventions to have unit costs already approved under other existing schemes.
19.	Block Resource Centres/ Cluster Resource Centres	• BRC/CRC to be located in school campus as far as possible. • Rs. 6 lakh ceiling for BRC building construction wherever required • Rs. 2 lakh for CRC construction wherever required - should be used as an additional classroom in schools. • Total cost of non-school (BRC and CRC) construction in any district should not exceed 5% of the overall projected expenditure under the programme in any year.

(Contd.)

(*Contd.*)

	Intervention	*Norm*
		• Deployment of up to 20 teacher in a block with more than 100 schools; 10 teachers in smaller Blocks in BRCs/CRCs. • Provision of furniture, etc. @ Rs. 1 lakh for a BRC and Rs. 10,000 for a CRC • Contingency grant of Rs. 12,500 for a BRC and Rs. 2500 for a CRC, per year • Identification of BRC/CRC personnel after intensive selection process in the preparatory phase itself.
20.	Interventions for out of school children	• As per norms already approved under Education Guarantee Scheme & Alternative and Innovative Education, providing for the following kind of interventions • Setting up Education Guarantee Centres in unserved habitations • Setting up other alternative schooling models • Bridge Courses, remedial courses, Back-to-School Camps with a focus on mainstreaming out of school children into regular schools.
21.	Preparatory activities for microplanning, household surveys, studies, community mobilization, school-based activities, office equipment, training and orientation at all levels, etc.	• As per specific proposal of a district, duly recommended by the State. Urban areas, within a district or metropolitan cities may be treated as a separate unit for planning as required.

The education system does not function in isolation from the society of which it is a part. Our social system is stratified into manifold layers based on class, caste, gender, and religion. Unequal social, economic and power equations, which persist, deeply influence children's access to education and their participation in the learning process. This is evident in the disparities in education access and attainment between different social and economic groups. Thus, girls belonging to SC, ST and Muslim minority communities, and children with disabilities, especially those from poor families, are educationally most vulnerable. The Right of Children to Free and Compulsory Education Act, 2009. In August 2009, Parliament passed the historic Right of Children to Free and Compulsory Education (RTE) Act, 2009. The new law must be seen from the perspective of children. It provides a justifiable legal framework that entitles all children between the ages of 6-14 years to an education of reasonable quality, based on principles of equity and non-discrimination. It provides for children's right to free and compulsory admission, attendance and completion of elementary education. More importantly, it provides for the child's right to education that is free from fear, stress and anxiety.

RASHTRIYA MADHYAMIK SHIKSHA ABHIYAN (RMSA)

RMSA is a Scheme for Universalisation of Access to and Improvement of Quality at the Secondary and Higher Secondary Stage. It is well recognized that eight years of education are insufficient to equip a child for the world of work as also to be a competent adult and citizen. The pressure on Secondary Education is already being felt due to the success of SSA. Therefore, while Secondary Education is not constitutionally compulsory, it is necessary and desirable that access to Secondary Education is universalized leading to enhanced participation and its quality is improved for all.

Vision

The vision for secondary education is to make good quality education available, accessible and affordable to all young persons in the age group of 14-18 years. With this vision in mind, the following is to be achieved

- To provide a Secondary school within 5 kms and Higher Secondary school within 7-10 kms,
- Ensure universal access of secondary education by 2017,
- Universal retention by 2020, and
- Providing access to secondary education with special references to economically weaker sections of the society, the educationally backward, the girls and the disabled children residing in rural areas and other marginalized categories like SC, ST, OBC and Educationally Backward Minorities.

Objectives

- To ensure that all secondary schools have physical facilities, staffs and supplies at least according to the prescribed standards through financial support in case of Government/Local Body and Government Aided Schools and appropriate regulatory mechanism in the case of other schools.
- To improve access to secondary schooling to all young persons according to norms-through proximate location (say Secondary school within 5 kms and Higher Secondary School within 7-10 kms), efficient and safe transport arrangements/residing facilities, depending on local circumstances including open schooling. However in hilly and difficult areas these norms can be relaxed. Preferably residential schools may be set up in such areas.
- To ensure that no child is deprived of secondary education of satisfactory quality due to gender, socio economic, disability and other barriers.
- To improve quality of secondary education resulting in enhanced intellectual, social and cultural learning.
- To ensure that all students pursuing secondary education receive education of good quality.
- Achievement of the above objectives would also, inter-alia, signify substantial progress in the direction of the common schooling system.

Important physical facilities provided under the scheme are:

(i) Additional class rooms, (ii) Laboratories, (iii) Libraries, (iv) Art and crafts room, (v) Toilet blocks, (vi) Drinking water provisions and (vii) Residential Hostels for Teachers in remote areas.

Important quality interventions provided under the scheme are:

(i) appointment of additional teachers to reduce PTR to 30:1, (ii) focus on Science, Math and English education, (iii) In-service training of teachers, (iv) science laboratories, (v) ICT enabled education, (vi) curriculum reforms; and (vii) teaching learning reforms.

Important equity interventions provided in the scheme are:

(i) special focus in micro planning, (ii) preference to Ashram schools in upgradation, (iii) preference to areas with concentration of SC/ST/Minority for opening of schools, (iv) special enrolment drive for the weaker section, (v) more female teachers in schools; and (vi) separate toilet blocks for girls.

Implementation Mechanism of the Scheme

The scheme is being implemented by the State government societies established for implementation of the scheme. The central share is released to the implementing agency directly. The applicable State share is also released to the implementing agency by the respective State Governments.

RIGHT TO EDUCATION ACT

The Right of Children to Free and Compulsory Education Act came into force from April 1, 2010. This was a historic day for the people of India as from this day the right to education is accorded the same legal status as the right to life as provided by Article 21A of the Indian Constitution. Every child in the age group of 6-14 years will be provided 8 years of elementary education in an age appropriate classroom in the vicinity of his/her neighbourhood. Any cost that prevents a child from accessing school will be borne by the State which shall have the responsibility of enrolling the child as well as ensuring attendance and completion of 8 years of schooling. No child shall be denied admission for want of documents; no child shall be turned away if the admission cycle in the school is over and no child shall be asked to take an admission test. Children with disabilities will also be educated in the mainstream schools. It was emphasized that it is important for the country, if we nurture our children and young people with the right education, India's future as a strong and prosperous country is secure.

The Act serves as a building block to ensure that every child has his or her right (as an entitlement) to get a quality elementary education, and that the State, with the help of families and communities, fulfils this obligation.

Few countries in the world have such a national provision to ensure both free and child-centred, child-friendly education. Central and state governments shall share financial responsibility for RTE. The central government shall prepare estimates of expenditures. State governments will be provided a percentage of these costs.

The Central Government may request the Finance Commission to consider providing additional resources to a state in order to carry out the provisions of RTE. The state government shall be responsible for providing the remaining funds needed to implement. There will be a funding gap which needs to be supported by partners from civil society, development agencies, corporate organisations and citizens of the country.

All schools will have to prescribe to norms and standards laid out in the Act and no school that does not fulfill these standards within 3 years will be allowed to function. All private schools will have to apply for recognition, failing which they will be penalized to the tune of ₹ 1 lakh and if they still continue to function will be liable to pay ₹ 10,000 per day as fine. Norms and standards of teacher qualification and training are also being laid down by an Academic Authority. Teachers in all schools will have to subscribe to these norms within 5 years.

The National Commission for Protection of Child Rights (NCPCR) has been mandated to monitor the implementation of this historic Right. A special Division within NCPCR will undertake this huge and important task in the coming months and years. A special toll free helpline to register complaints will be set up by NCPCR for this purpose. NCPCR welcomes the formal notification of this Act and looks forward to playing an active role in ensuring its successful implementation. NCPCR also invites all civil society groups, students, teachers, administrators, artists, writers, government personnel, legislators, members of the judiciary and all other stakeholders to join hands and work together to build a movement to ensure that every child of this country is in school and enabled to get at least 8 years of quality education.

Benefits of Right to Education Act, 2009—RTE has been a part of the directive principles of the State Policy under Article 45 of the Constitution, which is part of Chapter 4 of the Constitution. And rights in Chapter 4 are not enforceable. For the first time in the history of India we have made this right enforceable by putting it in Chapter 3 of the Constitution as Article 21. This entitles children to have the right to education enforced as a fundamental right.

There are several provisions in the Act, including for example, provisions prohibiting corporal punishment, detention and expulsion which need to be fore-fronted to ensure that we move towards a system that, as the National Policy on Education states, provides *'a warm, welcoming and encouraging approach for children to learn'* (NPE, 1986/92). The most important aspect, however, is to ensure that the teaching-learning process is free from stress and anxiety (Sec. 29), with obvious implications for curricular reform. Testing and school grading systems need to be reviewed to motivate children to deepen and widen their learning. The RTE Act also lays down the responsibilities of teachers. Teacher accountability systems would need to ensure that children are learning and that their right to learning in an environment that is free from stress and anxiety is not violated. The RTE Act provides for:

(i) The right of children to free and compulsory education till completion of elementary education in a neighborhood school.

(ii) It clarifies that 'compulsory education' means obligation of the appropriate government to provide free elementary education and ensure compulsory admission, attendance and completion of elementary education to every child in the six to fourteen age group. 'Free' means that no child shall be liable to pay any kind of fee or charges or expenses which may prevent him or her from pursuing and completing elementary education.

(iii) It makes provisions for a non-admitted child to be admitted to an age appropriate class.

(iv) It specifies the duties and responsibilities of appropriate Governments, local authority and parents in providing free and compulsory education, and sharing of financial and other responsibilities between the Central and State Governments.

(v) It lays down the norms and standards relating to, *inter alia*, Pupil Teacher Ratios (PTRs), buildings and infrastructure, school working days, teacher working hours.

(vi) It provides for rational deployment of teachers by ensuring that the specified pupil teacher ratio is maintained for each school, rather than just as an average for the State or District or Block, thus ensuring that there is practically no urban-rural imbalance in teacher postings. It also prohibits deployment of teachers for non-educational work, other than decennial census, elections to local authority, state legislatures and parliament, and disaster relief.

(vii) It provides for appointment of appropriately trained teachers, i.e. teachers with the requisite training and academic qualifications.

(viii) For children in 6-14 age group it prohibits (a) physical punishment and mental harassment, (b) screening procedures for admission, (c) capitation fees, (d) private tuition by teachers, (e) running of schools without recognition,

(ix) It provides for the following penalties:

(a) For charging capitation fee: fine upto 10 times the capitation fee charged;

(b) For resorting to screening during admission: ₹ 25,000 for first contravention; ₹ 50,000 for each subsequent contravention; and

(c) For running a school without recognition: fine up to ₹ one lakh, and in case of continuing contravention ₹ 10,000 for each day during which the contravention continues.

(x) It provides for development of curriculum in consonance with the values enshrined in the Constitution, and which would ensure the all round development of the child, building on the child's knowledge, potentiality and talent and making the child free of fear, trauma and anxiety through a system of child friendly and child centred learning.

(xi) It provides for protection and monitoring of the child's right to free and compulsory education and redressal of grievances by the National and State Commissions for Protection of Child Rights, which shall have the powers of a civil court.

School Access and Existing SSA Provisions for School Access

Universal access to schooling requires schooling facilities within reasonable reach of all children. If schools are not located in or near the habitations where children reside, they are unlikely to enroll in schools or continue schooling, even if they are formally enrolled in such schools. RTE Act provides that children are entitled to access elementary schools within "defined area or limits of neighbourhood".

Social access to schooling is as important as physical access. In a country with tremendous diversity in terms of language, caste, socio economic status, etc., it is important to ensure that the school recognizes these differences. If the language of instruction in a school in a tribal area is the State language, from class I itself, then the child is likely to find the school environment alienating. If teachers in the school have not been sensitized to actively dispel traditional perceptions regarding gender or caste roles, they are unlikely to take measures which would help girl students and children from marginalised communities to pursue education which is equitable and free of anxiety. The teachers' own patterns of communication with children, the seating arrangements in the classroom, allocation of work between children, can serve to reinforce (or dispel) societal perceptions about the 'proper' role and place of girls and SC/ST and minority community students.

Government schools have a high proportion of first generation school goers and children from marginalized communities. Teachers need to be sensitive to the fact that the home environments of many of these children do not facilitate homework or revision of school work. If these 'lapses' by the child are punished or the school does not help such children cope with studies, the child is likely to feel discouraged and drop out of formal schooling. The curriculum and textbooks also need to be intrinsically connected with the child's life outside the school, and need to reinforce the child's pride in her language, society and way of life, at the same time affording opportunities for learning about the wider world.

Thus, ensuring access to schooling is a wider challenge and is not confined merely to opening schools in or near the habitations where children reside. SSA provides for opening of new primary and upper primary schools as per State norms, to ensure that all children have access to primary school within one kilometer of their habitation and to an upper primary school, within three kilometers of the habitation.

Centres under the Education Guarantee Scheme (EGS) are intended to provide access to formal schooling, through a regular curriculum and textbooks, to children in habitations that do not qualify for a regular school due to existing state norms for opening schools. Often, EGS centres are sanctioned in remote habitations with few children, with the expectation that the State will alter its norms for opening schools and upgrade these EGS centres to regular schools within 2 years. Alternative and Innovative Education (AIE) centres are intended for children in difficult circumstances, with no regular schooling experience or whose schooling has been disrupted (street children, children from migrant families. Children with special needs, children who have never enrolled or dropped out of schooling).

AIE centres prepare them to attend formal schools within a short period of 9 months to a year. These centres transact a specially tailored curriculum and pedagogic practices that seek to impart the required age/grade specific knowledge and skills, so that the child is ready to enroll in a regular school and continue her studies there.

Girls from SC/ST and minority communities and from families below poverty line, face greater challenges in continuing education after the primary stage. Residential schools for such girls are provided at the upper primary level under SSA. These schools are opened in educationally backward blocks, with low levels of female literacy.

PRE-SCHOOL EDUCATION

Pre-school or Early Childhood Education (ECE) has, in recent years, been receiving a great deal of attention in research and policy circles. In our country also, this deficiency has received attention of educational thinkers and planners. The reasons being (a) a growing consensus among educationists that this stage of a child's education is crucial to future levels of learning; (b) the neglect of pre-school education component in ICDS centres; and c) gradual decline of schemes of other than ICDS for pre-school child development. While article 45 of the Constitution stipulates universal education to all children upto the age of 14 years, the division between Departments of Education and Women and Children has imposed a line between the age groups 0-6 years and 6-14 years. Unfortunately, the only programme of significance for pre-school education instituted by government is the Integrated

Child Development Services (ICDS) that has for various reasons focused on the nutrition and health aspects of children to the neglect of preschool education. For its part Ministry of Human Resource Development has made its position clear in relevant documents.

Government's resolve to give importance to pre-primary education can be traced back to the various reports and policy pronouncements after Independence. This was a major concern behind establishment of the Central Social Welfare Board (1958). The Education Commission (1964-66) underscored the importance of early child development as a strategy of child development per se, as well as an important input for enrolment and retention of children in primary schools. The committee on early child development headed by Ms. Mina Swaminathan (1972-73), while laying emphasis on preprimary education called for an integrated approach to child development. The National Policy on Education and Programme of Action (1986-92) had a distinct section/chapter on Early Childhood Care & Education. The Policy stipulates a "high priority" to ECCE "both as a feeder and a strengthening factor for primary education". POA called for universalization of ICDS by the year 2000 and widening the scope of anganwadis to include crèches. It also laid emphasis on participation of parents and improved training of anganwadi workers.

Right to Education and the Pre-School Component

The Right to Education Act, 2009 confines the right to education to the age group 6-14 years, keeping pre-school education outside its ambit. This has understandably led to some consternation among educationists as they see preschool education as a necessary building block to a child's transition to primary school. They argue that all evidence supports the need for a sound pre-school education programme for all children. A child that does not undergo a programme of early childhood learning, it is argued, particularly if he/she belongs to first-learner family, has difficulty in learning at the primary level and may end up being either a slow learner or even dropping out of the system early on. The high rates of drop-out witnessed in the first two years are cited as evidence of this lack of "school readiness" among children. In other words, if a child is to be enabled to attend and successfully complete the entire cycle of elementary education, as promised by the Act, she must be able to access a pre-school education programme of reasonable quality.

Section 11 of the RTE Act makes a provision for being engaged with preschool education. It states:

> "With a view to prepare children above the age of three years for elementary education and to provide early childhood care and education for all children until they complete the age of six years, the appropriate Government may make necessary arrangement for providing free pre-school education for such children"

This allows for the necessary space within the ambit of the RTE Act to enable a greater degree of involvement in the pre-school segment of education. Indeed, universalization of pre-primary education should be treated as a prerequisite for achieving the goals of the RTE Act.

Recommendations for Pre-School Education

The Supreme Court has ordered in Writ Petition no. 196 of 2001, *People's Union of Civil Liberties v/s. Union of India and Others*, that the benefits of the scheme of ICDS (and some other benefits available to children) shall be legal entitlements. This interim order has been cited by the Working Group on Children Under Six constituted at the request of the Planning Commission. We find ourselves in agreement with the recommendations of this Working Group as published in Economic and Political Weekly, December 29, 2007 and recommend that they should also be treated as a part of the strategy for implementation of RTE Act.

Recommendations of the Working Group are of far-reaching importance for future of early child development. In one of the significant sections it states:

> "The care of young children cannot be left to the family alone—it is also a social responsibility. Social intervention is required, both in the form of enabling parents to take better care of their children at home, and in the form of direct provision of health, nutrition, pre-school education

PSE and related services. Interventions for children under six years or ECCD must broadly address at least three dimensions: child health, child development and education and child nutrition. These must necessarily be provided simultaneously in the same system of care".

Some of the important recommendations of this Working Group, which need to be fully implemented during are as follows:

(i) **Rights Approach:** This framework recognizes that childcare, healthcare, nutrition, and PSE development are basic rights of all Indian children.

(ii) **Age-specific Interventions:** Attention has to be paid to the varying requirements of different age group (specifically, zero to six months, six months to three years, and three to six years), and to the need for corresponding interventions.

(iii) **Convergence:** Effective strategies for children under six require active "convergence" between core programmes, especially ICDS, the NRHM and Sarva Shiksha Abhiyan.

(iv) **Decentralization:** A decentralized approach is required, fostering participatory planning, community ownership, responsiveness to local circumstances, and the involvement of panchayati raj institutions.

(v) **Community Action:** Various forms of community action need to be promoted. These include monitoring and supporting the local anganwadi, selection and evaluation of anganwadi workers, participatory planning, use of untied grants, etc.

(vi) **Capacity-Building:** Major investment in capacity-building and training are required at all levels, all the more so as ECCD is poorly understood. Programmes of such scale and complexity as ICDS cannot succeed without extensive investments in improving management skills and practices.

(vii) **Universalization with Quality:** "Universalization with quality" should be the overarching goal for ICDS in the Eleventh Plan. This would include raising the number of anganwadis to a minimum of 14 lakh (with priority to disadvantaged groups), extending all ICDS services to all children under six and all eligible women, and improving the quality of services.

(viii) Pre-school Education: For children aged three to six years, pre-school education should be the primary focus of ICDS activities. Aside from adoption of the two-worker model, this requires appropriate training, infrastructure, equipment, supervision and support.

GIRLS' EDUCATION

The National Policy on Education and the POA (1986/92) brought the issue of gender and girls education centre stage. More, importantly it linked education of women and girls to their empowerment. NPE states that education should be a transformative force, build women's self-confidence, improve their position in society and challenge inequalities. It states: *Education shall be used as an agent of basic change in the status of women. In order to neutralize accumulated distortions of the past, there will be a well-conceived edge in favour of women. The national education system will play a positive, interventionist role in the empowerment of women (NPE 1986)*. This vision remains the overarching framework for programme and policy development.

The RTE in different sections makes reference to gender and girls education both explicitly and implicitly. Some of the relevant provisions are—no discrimination against children from 'disadvantaged groups and `weaker sections' on any grounds (including gender); inclusion of women in school monitoring committees; provision of good quality education that includes equity issues, curriculum development in conformity with constitutional stipulations, training, enrolment in age appropriated classes (which will largely apply to girls, especially from disadvantaged communities).

Bridging the gender and social gap is one of the four goals of SSA. The programme has undertaken several measures to improve girls' access to schooling and retention and more recently on addressing issues of quality and equity. Some of the important measures have been—the formulation and implementation of two targeted schemes (NPEGEL and KGBV), improving the school infrastructure and providing support (e.g. free textbooks, uniforms etc.) to girls especially from disadvantaged communities appointment of female teachers, training of teachers on gender issues and assigning gender focal points. Being one of the goals of SSA there has been regular monitoring and reporting on the progress being made on gender and girls education.

SPECIAL SCHEMES FOR GIRLS

Within the ambit of SSA two special schemes—KGBV and NPEGEL have been effective in building an environment for girls' education. The targeted approach of these programmes has been particularly useful in reaching out to girls from marginalized communities. Below are some suggestion for further improving these schemes so that they contribute significantly to meeting the needs and challenges of RTE.

Kasturba Gandhi Balika Vidyalayas KGBV

The importance of the KGBV Scheme in addressing the educational needs of girls from marginalized communities has been highlighted in various reviews. Given the importance of the scheme the following could be considered:

(i) Norms and guidelines of KGBV—financial, physical and other members, including design, be revisited and revised appropriately.
(ii) KGBVs run by MS and NGOs are particularly successful as they augment resources to bring in empowerment-oriented content. The scheme should make adequate provisions to enable such interventions on a wider and sustained basis.
(iii) Strengthening of the role of the National Resource Group (NRG) and other experts and organizations with expertise in various aspects of girls education in providing academic and other support to KGBV
(iv) There are reports that persons responsible for admission to KGBVs are so keen to have full enrolment that they seldom keep in view the categories of girls for whom these institutions have been established. Work needs to be done in this regard.
(v) Development of an appropriate curriculum framework,

teaching-learning material, teacher training programmes and monitoring and assessment mechanisms keeping in mind the contexts, and age of the learners and the residential nature of the scheme be taken up urgently by the appropriate authorities with the involvement of experienced organizations, especially with a strong gender orientation.

The National Programme for Education of Girls at Elementary Level

The National Programme for Education of Girls at Elementary Level (NPEGEL) by ensuring targeted resources over a number of years has contributed to the progress in the area of girls' education. Various reviews have identified some of the concerns related to the scheme as being uneven quality; fragmented approach where activities are picked up from the indicative list and do not form a cohesive strategy; overlap of activities with other components of the scheme such as the AIE component; local planning not strong enough; activities/strategies related to gender have remained an add- on and not mainstreamed; no review of quality of modules etc. being produced; insufficient impact of the gender training programmes on making classroom practices more gender sensitive; impact of the model cluster school is not certain; etc.

The scheme could be revised to address some of the problems mentioned above and to bring it in line with the provisions of the RTE. Some of the areas where modifications can be considered are as follows:

(i) Scope: In order to respond to new realities could include blocks with high migration.
(ii) Some modifications can be thought of in the planning process. In keeping with the RTE school development plans can be amalgamated at the cluster and then block. The existing school based structures, along with the local authorities could be involved in the planning process.
(iii) In order to lessen fragmentation, the plans should, along with the strategies and outcomes, also mention the rationale for taking up a particular activity and mention what problem it hopes to address. At present the programme has a little bit of everything and therefore the impact gets dissipated.
(iv) The programmes being planned could be more focused

on developing the 'special training' component mentioned in the RTE as well as short camps aimed at empowering girls through building their selfconfidence, self-esteem etc. Such programmes could focus on developing leadership skills of these girls. The content and pedagogy of such interventions could be developed with the support of organizations with experience in this area. The focus of the empowerment related special programmes could aim at supporting older girls.

(v) The component of training of the representatives from community structures and school level forums on gender and social equity issues could be strengthened.

Mahila Samakhya

Mahila Samakhya (MS) programme was started nearly 20 years ago and has been recognized as an effective strategy for creating circumstances for girls' education and empowerment. The critical thing in this programme is that its agenda and priorities are set by women's groups, called Mahila Sanghas, themselves. At the time when this programme was started questions were raised whether it would in fact contribute to girls' education. Over the years Mahila Sanghas and their federations have themselves give a place of importance to girls' education. They play an active role in working towards removal of barriers to the participation of girls in education. They do this through a four-pronged strategy:

(i) By running preparatory non-formal centres, such as Jagjagi Kendras in Bihar;

(ii) By working towards change in popular perception about the status of girls in family as well as in the community—rather than mere housewives to active citizens and workers, no different from males. This in turn motivates parents to send their daughters to schools;

(iii) By actively working for enrolment and retention of children in schools, especially never-enrolled and dropout girls. In some districts where Mahila Samakhya is being implemented, they have built widespread awareness resulting in a veritable movement for improvement of girls' education.

(iv) By running of Mahila Shikshan Vihars where adolescent girls receive elementary education and go through processes for empowerment.

Simultaneously the Mahila Sanghas ensure that the education system is sensitive to the needs and interests of girls—through monitoring and ensuring accountability in village schools, addressing teacher absenteeism, MDM implementation and quality, etc. Mahila Samakhya has demonstrated the possibilities and practicable ways of creating and using gender-sensitive curriculum, classroom pedagogy, teacher training and life-skills. Sangha women are often members of village level committees, and play an important role in SSA implementation and monitoring.

This spirit of MS and the overall tenor of the RTE provide enormous scope for synergic outputs. Special mention in this regard should be made of the fact that occasionally one hears of MS being expected to subserve the goals of SSA. This would not be in accordance with the stipulation of 1986 Education Policy. MS should continue to jealously adhere to its non-negotiable principles, including the stipulation which gives to them space for making their own decisions regarding programme priorities and implementation strategies. Secondly, Mahila Shikshan Vihars have demonstrated ability to run bridge courses and to develop necessary curricula and teaching-learning arrangements. They could make an important contribution in conducting programmes for children who get admitted to age appropriate classes but require preparatory courses to keep pace with other students.

CHILDREN WITH SPECIAL NEEDS

I. Approach and Coverage

The SSA scheme covers *all* children in 6-14 years age group. The SSA Framework of Implementation explicitly states: *"SSA will ensure that every child with special needs, irrespective of the kind, category and degree of disability, is provided education in an appropriate environment. SSA will adopt 'zero rejection' policy so that no child is left out of the education system"*. The RTE Act 2009, in section 3(1) entitles *all* children in the 6-14 years age group to a right to free and compulsory elementary education in a neighborhood school.

II. Coverage of Children with Disabilities within the RTE Act

Children with disabilities have not been explicitly included as a category in section 2(d) of the RTE Act, which otherwise lists children belonging to disadvantaged groups. However, the same section also allows the appropriate government to specify, by notification, any other group of children who are disadvantaged as a result of any other factor. Thus, appropriate governments can issue a notification in section 2(d) of the RTE Act to include children with disabilities, within the category of 'children belonging to disadvantaged groups'.

Section 3(2) of the Act qualifies that only a child suffering from disability as defined under clause (i) of section (2) of the PWD Act, 1996 shall have a right to pursue free and compulsory elementary education in accordance with provisions of chapter V of the said Act. The PWD Act, 1996 excludes children suffering from certain disabilities such as cerebral palsy, autism and learning disabilities like dyslexia, disprasia etc. Further, chapter V of the PWD Act 1996 permits a multi option model for education of CWSN, which includes 'special schools' etc.

Educational Placement

An inclusive space for education of *all* children should be made available and appropriate strategies need to be followed. The SSA Framework provides that *'as far as possible every child with special needs should be placed in regular schools, with needed support services'*. Under SSA, a wide range of options for educational services have been given, including for example, open school, non-formal and alternative schooling, distance education, special schools and home-based education. This range of options and strategies should be reviewed in the context of the RTE Act, which entitles all children to elementary education in regular schools that meet the norms and standards specified in the Schedule to the Act.

Children with disabilities need to be facilitated to acquire certain skills that will enable them to access elementary education as envisaged in the Act. For instance, they may need mobility training, training in Braille, sign language, tactile sign-language, postural training, etc. Thus, 'school preparedness' of children with disabilities must be ensured by providing 'special training' as envisaged under section 4 of the RTE Act. This training may be residential, non residential or even home based, as per their specific requirements.

The existing non formal and alternate schooling (including home based education) options for children with disabilities can be recast as 'special training'. This means that (a) all children with special needs who are not enrolled in schools or have dropped out, will first be enrolled in a neighbourhood school in an age appropriate grade, (b) they will be entitled to 'special training' through regular teachers or teachers specifically appointed for the purpose. In the case of CWSN, the state may appoint a person with degree/diploma in special education as a resource teacher, who will impart special training to children with special needs. The resource teacher may be posted at the block or cluster level and can operate in an itinerant mode, covering a group of schools where children with special needs are enrolled.

The reason for appointing the resource teacher for a group of schools rather than in every school is because the number of children with special needs in any single school would be quite small, as children with special needs comprise only about 2% of the 6-14 years population, and because there may be several schools in which no children with special needs are enrolled.

Moreover, in the near future qualified special needs teachers would not be available. The training can be residential (including home based, depending on the nature and degree of disability and kind of support required) or non residential. The duration of the training can be from three months to two years.

After completion of special training, children with special needs will continue regular classes in the age appropriate grade in which they have been enrolled. They will continue to receive special attention even after completion of 'special training' for their successful academic and emotional integration in the class. 'Special schools' will have to become inclusive schools (neighbourhood schools). They will continue to function as resource centres for special inputs to regular and resource teachers, for teaching of children with special needs. The nature of this resource support can cover aspects like teacher training, development of appropriate syllabi and textbooks for children with special needs, development of individualized education plans and assessment methods, appropriate TLMs etc. Special schools would simultaneously need to work towards becoming inclusive neighbor hood schools.

CURRICULUM AND EVALUATION

Content and Process of Learning in RTE Act

RTE Act mentions eight factors which should be taken into consideration by the designated academic authority to lay down the curriculum and the evaluation procedure. These eight factors are: conformity with Constitutional values; all-round development of the child; building-up the child's knowledge, potentiality and talent; development of physical and mental abilities to the fullest extent; learning through activities, discovery and exploration in a child friendly and child-centred manner; the child's mother tongue serving 'as far as practicable' as the medium of instruction; making the child free of fear, trauma and anxiety and helping the child to express views freely; and comprehensive and continuous evaluation of the child's understanding of knowledge and the ability to apply it. These factors can be deemed to provide a fairly comprehensive coverage of the indicators of a child-centred curricular policy for the elementary stage of education. Some of these factors have been a part of the various guidelines prepared under Central and State-level programmes launched over more than two decades since the formulation of the National Policy of Education, 1986.

Quality Concerns

Concern for improving the quality of education has been growing increasingly stronger. But the gap between expectation and actual performance in terms of children's learning, especially in the case of those disadvantaged by physical and social circumstances, continues to remain. It is not as if no efforts are being made to address the critical issue of quality. If anything, under SSA most states have rolled out a variety of interventions, from pilot programmes within the Learning Enhancement Programme (LEP) to teacher training, material development, specific subject-oriented programmes, etc.

Textbooks

The textbooks from class I-VIII prepared by NCERT under this syllabus NCF- 2005 are a paradigm shift in addressing the concerns expressed by the NCF-2005 and mandated by the RTE Act. Many States have adopted the NCERT textbooks, but in the transition from SSA to full scale implementation of RTE, it is imperative that States prepare textbooks in tune with the NCF-2005 constructivist approach that reflect the socio-cultural and geographical diversity, prevalent in the State. National agencies like the NCERT would therefore have to play a major role in enhancing the capacity of State agencies to undertake this task. State Governments shall have to put into place institutional mechanisms whereby different agencies charged with the responsibility of curriculum development, syllabi, textbook writing, textbook production and teacher training work together in order to fulfill the mandatory requirements of the RTE Act in relation to content and process. It may also be desirable for the State Governments to review such agencies in order that they may be re-structured in the light of the tasks outlined by the RTE Act.

COMPREHENSIVE AND CONTINUOUS EVALUATION

The term 'Comprehensive and Continuous Evaluation' (CCE) essentially means that evaluation should be treated as an integral part of teaching rather than as an event which follows the completion of teaching. The prevailing examination system treats evaluation as a means of judging and passing a verdict. Such a practice is incompatible with the concept of child-centred education. Moreover, with the formulation of RTE, evaluation in any form, including examination, cannot be treated as a basis for stopping a child from progressing to the next Class. In the prevailing system, examination is used for eliminating children who are found to be weak on the basis of their poor marks. Once declared 'fail', they either repeat grade (i.e. stagnate) or leave the school altogether. Compelling a child to repeat a class by studying the same syllabus for one whole year is a form of wastage of resources on which many educational planners, including the late J.P. Naik, have elaborately commented. Sufficient evidence exists to show that a child who is asked to repeat the same Class does not necessarily develop any new capacities for negotiating the syllabus of that class and in most cases such children feel discouraged and defeated. Parents of such children also tend to view them as being fit for failure, thereby reinforcing the perception which the school has already used for declaring the child 'fail' on the basis of a three-hour test.

Comprehensive Evaluation

Modern educational theory has battled with such obsolete practices for a longtime. Its message is simple and clear: namely that children's learning and development cannot be viewed in terms of a rigidly defined class-structure structure, nor it can be fitted into an annual cycle of evaluation and promotion. The RTE Act represents the legal approval of modern educational thinking when the Act prohibits stagnation and requires that a child can join the school at any point in the year. The vision underlying the RTE Act is further clarified by the prohibition imposed on Board examination at the end of the elementary stage or before it. This vision is completely consistent with NCF which also recommends that there should be no Board examination at any point in elementary education. Taking this larger picture into account we can infer that CCE has been included in RTE as a means of overcoming and going beyond the rigidities and harshness of the prevailing conventional examination and testing system in elementary classes. To be more precise 'Continuous Evaluation' means that the teacher's work should be continuously guided by the child's response and participation in classroom activities. In other words, evaluation should be seen as a process whereby the teacher learns about the child in order to be able to teach better, and 'Continuous Evaluation' becomes a strategy of assessment which is a part and parcel of teaching itself.

Continuous Evaluation

The term 'Comprehensive' implies the capacity to view the child from a holistic perspective, rather than merely in terms of a learner of different school subjects. A comprehensive evaluation strategy would imply that aspects such as the child's health, personality, behaviour and attitude are also perceived in the context of development and growth. Conventionally these aspects are either neglected in our education system or as we now see in private schools, dealt with by using an arbitrarily devised grading system which conveys the impression that the teacher has judged the child according to a norm. It is the duty of the teacher to make every possible effort, through interaction and engagement, to observe and understand the child's own nature. It is also important that the teacher does not judge the child's nature. Rather, what is required is that the teacher notices the inherent potential of the child as a learner in the context of his or her nature. Such a view will help the teacher to devise appropriate methods by which the best potential inherent in the child's abilities can be drawn out and put to use. 'Comprehensive Evaluation', therefore, does not mean that each and every aspect of the child's behaviour, personality and attitude should be either measured or graded. Instead, it is expected that the teacher will first understand in a dynamic manner the different aspects of a child's evolving nature and then formulate his or her comments based on observations. Training for careful observation and recordkeeping will have to be organised and executed in a careful and academically sound manner to enable teachers to fulfil the expectation of the RTE Act. For guiding teachers to observe a child's behaviour and attitudes, a new initiative will have to be taken for developing relevant material which can serve as a basis for training programmes.

TEACHERS AND TEACHER TRAINING

RTE Provisions

Systemic conditions are greatly influenced by the quality of training with which teachers are inducted into the system, and the support given to them on a sustained basis to maintain their motivation and academic capacity. Although professional teacher education programmes have existed in the country for over a century, their basic features in terms of theoretical premises, content and substance, experiences offered and modalities of transaction have by and large remained unchanged.

The RTE Act attaches immense significance to the role of teachers in reforming elementary education. Section 23 highlights the need for making available professionally trained teachers for the school system; however it also recognises that some States may not have the capacity for professional training of teachers in the numbers required and provides that the Central Government may relax the requirement of professional training for a period not exceeding five years, within which period all teachers would need to acquire the prescribed qualifications. Section 24 specifies the academic duties of teachers, including *inter alia* timely completion of curriculum, providing additional support to children, where required, and maintaining contact with the parents of children. Section 26 lays down that the prescribed pupil teacher ratio shall be maintained for each school.

Infrastructure

Section 19 of the RTE Act states that "No school shall be established or recognised under section 18, unless it fulfils the norms and standards specified in the schedule." Minimum required school infrastructure has been defined for the first time in the RTE Act, such as an all weather building consisting of at least one classroom for every teacher and an office-cum-store-cum HM room, separate toilets for boys and girls, safe and adequate drinking water facilities for all children, barrier free access, boundary wall or green fencing, kitchen for cooking MDM, a library, playground etc. It implies that all schools should be composite schools, i.e., they should have all these facilities within three years of the coming into force of the RTE Act. All new schools that are constructed after the three year period would need to provide all facilities upfront, as graded augmentation of school infrastructure to meet the RTE requirements, will not be permissible under the Act. Recognition of existing schools that do not meet the infrastructure requirements within the specified period will be withdrawn. New schools will not be recognised and permitted to function until they provide at least the infrastructure specified in the schedule to the Act.

Existing pool of school infrastructure is of variable quality. DISE data (2007-08) states that 5.12 per cent of all government schools do not have school buildings. 13.78 per cent government elementary schools in rural areas do not have drinking water facilities and 54.57 per cent do not have separate toilets. Only 33 of schools have electricity. Also, schools generally do not have appropriate barrier free features. The ramps, even if available, are often too steep and do not allow easy access for children with special needs (CWSN) It is clear that up gradation of school infrastructure will be an important task to be accomplished within three years of the commencement of the Act.

Existing SSA Provisions

SSA provides buildings (with toilets, drinking water facilities, kitchen for MDM) for new primary and upper primary schools sanctioned under the Scheme. It also provides a classroom for every teacher or for every grade/class whichever is lower, in primary and upper primary schools with the provision that there would be two class rooms with a veranda to every primary school, with at least two teachers. It also provides for a room for the head-master in upper primary schools/sections. Facilities for drinking water and toilets in schools existing prior to SSA are provided only to urban schools that are not covered under the National Drinking Water Mission and Total Sanitation Campaign of the Ministry of Rural Development, GOI.

Need for Revision of SSA Provisions in Light of RTE Act

SSA civil works norms would need to be revised to ensure creation of school infrastructure at par with RTE requirements. A clear detailing of essential physical infrastructure in school buildings would help States in preparing appropriate proposals. SSA norms, at present, do not explicitly spell out the minimum required infrastructure in schools. The revised norms would have to provide for a classroom for every teacher and an office cum store cum HM room in primary schools. It would be advisable for MHRD to examine whether SSA can now support augmentation of infrastructure in schools that were opened by the State Governments prior to SSA or outside the Scheme of SSA. Many of these schools have infrastructure facilities lower than what is envisaged under SSA.

Incorporation of Child Friendly Elements in School Buildings

The quality of the school building and the design of its indoor and outdoor spaces plays an important role in shaping the child's perception of the attractiveness of the school as a learning and play space. Therefore, whether the child is motivated to enroll and thereafter continue to attend school on a regular basis, also depends on the quality of school buildings. Schools are built for children. School building designs should, therefore, respond to the needs of children. Different facilities in the school should be built to the scale of the children, such as drinking water taps and urinals, children's chalk boards, display and storage spaces in the classrooms, playgrounds and other outdoor and indoor spaces in the school premises.

SSA Provisions vis-à-vis RTE Norms

SSA goals include universal access and retention, bridging of gender and social category gaps in elementary education, and achieving significant enhancement in learning levels of children. SSA provides for a variety of activities in order to achieve its overall goals, including *inter alia*:

(i) Universal access through opening and construction new primary and upper primary schools in unserved areas, and opening centres under the Education Guarantee Scheme (EGS) and Alternative and Innovative Education (AIE) to enable hard-to-reach children mainstream into regular formal schools.

(ii) Universal retention through provisioning of teachers to achieve a pupil teacher ratio of 1:40 at the primary and 1:35 at the upper primary level, annual in-service teacher training, textbooks for children, support for adequate infrastructure through additional classroom, toilets (separate for girls) and drinking water.

(iii) Bridging gender and social category gaps through programmes of gender and caste sensitization of teachers, opening residential facilities through Kasturba Gandhi Balika Vidyalayas (KGBV) in educationally backward blocks, and implementing programmes under the National Programme for Education of Girls at Elementary Level (NPEGEL), which include community mobilisation as well as intensive teacher training.

(iv) Improving quality of education through introduction of

child friendly and child centred learning systems, and achievement testing of the child's understanding and learning.

Some of the provisions mandated under RTE exist under SSA or certain other schemes of the Department of School Education and Literacy such as provisions under the Teacher Education and Mid Day Meal schemes. Certain other provisions of RTE, such as drinking water and toilets for existing schools are sourced from Centrally Sponsored Schemes of other departments.

Provisions for uniforms, stationery, textbooks, transport are part of many State budgets and these will continue to be provided through State schemes. These provisions notwithstanding, additional resources would be required to meet certain provisions of the RTE Act, and SSA norms would require to be changed.

NATIONAL CURRICULUM FRAMEWORK

The National Curriculum Framework (NCF 2005) is one of four National Curriculum Frameworks published in 1975, 1988, 2000 and 2005 by the National Council of Educational Research and Training NCERT The document provides the framework for making syllabi, textbooks and teaching practices within the school education programmes in India.

The NCF 2005 document draws its policy basis from earlier government reports on education as Learning Without Burden and National Policy of Education 1986-1992 and focus group discussion. After wide ranging deliberations 21 National Focus Group Position Papers have been developed under the NCF-2005. The state of art position papers provided inputs for formulation of NCF-2005.

The document and its offshoot textbooks have come under different forms of reviews in the press. Its draft document came under the criticism from the Central Advisory Board of Education (CABE). In February 2008, the Director, Krishna Kumar in an interview also discussed the challenges that are faced by the document.

The approach and recommendations of NCF-2005 are for the entire educational system. A number of its recommendations, for example, focus on rural schools. The syllabus and textbooks based on it are being used by all the CBSE schools, but NCF-based material is also being used in many State schools.

NCF 2005 has been translated into 22 languages and has influenced the syllabii in 17 States. The NCERT gave a grant of ₹ 10 lakh to each State to promote NCF in the language of the State and to compare its current syllabus with the syllabus proposed, so that a plan for future reforms could be made. Several States have taken up this challenge. This exercise is being carried out with the involvement of State Councils for Educational Research and Training [SCERT] and District Institutes of Education and Training [DIETs].

District Institutes of Education and Training [DIETs]

The scheme to strengthen teacher education by establishing quality training institutions, such as, the District Institutes of Education and Training (DIETs) was initiated in 1987. The scheme proposed to create viable institutional, academic and technical resource base for orientations, training and continuous up-gradation of knowledge, competence and pedagogical skills of school teachers' in the country. The guidelines provided seven academic units with 22 faculty positions that cover different areas such as planning and management, education technology, material development etc. The DIETs are now twenty two years old but still many of them do not function as was envisaged in its guidelines.

REFERENCES

National Plan of Action India (2003). Department of Elementary Education and Literacy, MHRD, New Delhi.

Right to Education Act—2010. The Gazette of India, June 20, 2012, New Delhi.

Shah, J.P. (2012). How to fulfill the RTE Promise: New Delhi: *The Indian Express*.

Sarva Shiksha Abhiyan: A Programme for Universal Elementary Education (2002). Manual for Appraisal of Plans. New Delh: MHRD.

Sarva Shiksha Abhiyan: Programmes for Universal Elementary Education (2009). New Delhi: MHRD.

2

Elementary Education — International Scenario

INTRODUCTION

Universal Primary Education is one of the eight Millennium Development Goals and great improvements have been achieved in the past decade, yet a great deal remains to be done. Transparency International has identified corruption in the education sector as a major stumbling block to achieving Universal Primary Education in Africa. Furthermore, demand in the developing world for improved educational access is not as high as one would expect as governments avoid the recurrent costs involved and there is economic pressure on those parents who prefer their children making money in the short term over any long-term benefits of education.

Recent studies on child labor and poverty have suggested that when poor families reach a certain economic threshold where families are able to provide for their basic needs, parents return their children to school. This has been found to be true, once the threshold has been breached, even if the potential economic value of the children's work has increased since their return to school. But without capacity, there is no development. A study conducted by the UNESCO International Institute for Educational Planning indicates that stronger capacities in educational planning and management may have an important spill-over effect on the system as a whole. Sustainable capacity development requires complex interventions at the institutional, organizational and individual levels that could be based on the following foundational principles:

- national leadership and ownership should be the touchstone of any intervention;

- strategies must be context relevant and context specific;
- they should embrace an integrated set of complementary interventions, though implementation may need to proceed in steps;
- partners should commit to a long-term investment in capacity development, while working towards some short-term achievements; and
- outside intervention should be conditional on an impact assessment of national capacities at various levels.

Lack of good universities, and a low acceptance rate for good universities, is evident in countries with a high population density. In some countries, there are uniform, over structured, inflexible centralized programmes from a central agency that regulates all aspects of education.

India is now developing technologies that will skip land based telephone and internet lines. Instead, India launched EDUSAT, an education satellite that can reach more of the country at a greatly reduced cost. There is also an initiative started by the OLPC foundation, a group out of MIT Media Lab and supported by several major corporations to develop a $100 laptop to deliver educational software. Introduction of Aakash Tablet PCs will also bring about a major change in educational scenario. These will enable developing countries to give their children a digital education, and help close the digital divide across the world.

In Africa, the New Partnership for Africa's Development (NEPAD) has launched an "e-school programme" to provide all 600,000 primary and high schools with computer equipment, learning materials and internet access within 10 years. Private groups, like The Church of Jesus Christ of Latter-day Saints, are working to give more individual opportunities to receive education in developing countries through such programmes as the Perpetual Education Fund. An International Development Agency project called nabuur.com, started with the support of former American President Bill Clinton, uses the Internet to allow co-operation by individuals on issues of social development.

GOALS AND PURPOSES OF ELEMENTARY EDUCATION

Democratization of education is the evolution of education away from models intended to support ideological, social, or industrial systems toward open, universal public education. Great Britain demonstrates the evolution of open, democratic systems of European education since the Renaissance. Japan in Asia has redesigned its public education system since World War II to reflect those same open democratic values. Chile in South America is currently undergoing an aggressive democratization of public education. The similarities of the reforms in these nations parallels similar reforms underway in the United States.

United States: Throughout the history of the United States, Americans have expressed a desire for an educated citizenry. Efforts to establish or reform education in this country include the Old Deluder Satan Act, enacted in Massachusetts in 1647, Thomas Jefferson's 1779 Bill for the More General Diffusion of Knowledge, The Common School Movement of the 1800s, the Education for All American Youth initiative of 1944, and George W. Bush's No Child Left Behind Act of 2001. The existence of a cumulative and consecutive system of universal public education for young children is a part of the national heritage of the United States, and it is expected that elementary education will play a major role in preparing future citizens to live in a modern, industrialized, global society.

Control over elementary education is reserved to the states; however, in 1979 the U.S. Department of Education was created by President Jimmy Carter to coordinate, manage, and account for federal support of educational programmes. National and local attention continues to be directed at elementary education in the twenty-first century, as leaders, teachers, and parents seek ways to make the first step in the American education system educative, meaningful, and positive.

While current educational reforms reflect a myriad of societal changes, elementary education at the beginning of the new millennium still resembles the vernacular schools of colonial America. The essential skills of reading, writing, spelling, and arithmetic occupy center stage, and the "common school" moral themes of honesty, hard work, diligence, and application prevail.

In America, children normally enroll in elementary schools at age five or six and exit elementary school at age eleven or twelve. In 2002 approximately 25 million children attended elementary schools in the United States. Readiness for elementary school is viewed as highly important. Through Head Start programmes, the government provides educational opportunities for children from disadvantaged circumstances in order for them to be prepared for elementary school. Parents of the children who may not qualify for government-supported programmes often enroll their children in privately run preschools in hopes of setting their children on a successful path to elementary school. Although school attendance is not mandatory in most states until first grade, national surveys of parents of early elementary pupils show that 98 per cent of primary school children attend kindergarten before entering first grade.

The rapid changes in cognitive, social, and moral growth of an elementary school student makes the elementary classroom an ideal setting for shaping individual attitudes and behaviors. The elementary classroom may provide the best opportunity to set in place moral and ethical characteristics and understandings that have the potential to improve society. Children in the elementary schools are still malleable, and this emphasis on character education is seen as a particularly urgent matter in American classrooms. In fact, the socialization of children in America is no longer viewed as the sole responsibility of their parents.

The view of using the elementary classroom as a stage for molding future citizens of a democratic society is not new, but it does give rise to controversy regarding programmes and methods, as parents may disagree with specific curriculum being promoted by local, state, or national agencies. For example, sex education at the elementary school level has been the object of much debate among religious and special interest groups. One result of the disagreements over such controversial curricula may be the large number of children home schooled in 1999-2001 (estimated to be more than 1.3 million). Even so, support may still be offered to home-schooled students through curriculum, books, and materials provided by local schools or districts, as well as access to extracurricular activities and special classes in areas such as technology.

Europe: Elementary education in the United States has roots in European models of education, and, in fact, elementary education systems around the world share many common characteristics. Efforts to create public elementary school systems in Europe (mostly in the nineteenth century) were initiated by leaders in the national or central governments. Dominant political, social, and economic classes used elementary schools to encourage conformity with the ideas and values that perpetuated the status quo and provided little opportunity for upward socioeconomic mobility. In the twentieth century the requirement for a more educated workforce has enhanced the place of elementary education within the continuum of formerly hierarchical European education systems.

The compulsory age for children to begin elementary school is five or six and elementary education may last for six years. Typical subjects include reading, writing, arithmetic, art, geography, history, physical education, fine arts, and foreign languages. In some countries, non-compulsory religion classes may be offered. Since the fall of Communism, most eastern European elementary school systems follow the western European education model. Elementary schools in Europe experience many of the same issues related to student achievement, diversity, poverty, and violence that face their U.S. counterparts, and standardized testing has become increasingly important in many countries, such as Great Britain.

Asia (Japan): Elementary education in Japan is built on a model of communities of people working together to become healthy in mind, body, and spirit. Students are educated to respect the value of individuals, and to love truth and justice. Elementary education begins at age six in Japan and ends at age eleven or twelve. The structure of Japan's 6-3-3-4 school system was established by the School Education Law of 1947. The educational reforms resulting from this law, carried out under the direction of the American Occupation, decentralized control of education, authorized autonomous private schools, and encouraged the development of community education. The authority to establish schools is limited to the Ministry of Education, local governments, and private organizations that fulfill the requirements of becoming a school corporation. Municipalities are responsible for establishing elementary schools. Parents, especially mothers, take an active role in their children's education and reinforce the school curriculum through teaching their children at home or enrolling them in *Jukus,* which are privately run "cram" schools.

South America (Chile): Children in Chile attend primary (elementary) school for eight years. They study a curriculum and use textbooks approved by the government's Ministry of Education, though following the 1980 educational reforms the oversight of elementary education in Chile was transferred to municipal governments. The typical primary school curriculum includes reading, writing, mathematics, social studies, music, physical education, and art. A national programme of school breakfasts and lunches recognizes the importance of nutrition in the education of children. Chilean elementary education is faced with inequities in access to education among the rich and poor and a high dropout rate among the nation's poorest children. The National Council for School Aid and Grants is charged with making scholarships available to all children. Since 1988, the national government of Chile has provided support for private schools, and this has caused a downturn in public primary school enrollments.

EDUCATION IN DEVELOPING COUNTRIES—CERTAIN PROBLEMS

Around the world, about 75 million children—more than half of them girls—have no opportunity to attend primary school. One in three children in Africa that are enrolled in school drop out of primary education. For socially disadvantaged groups such as rural or indigenous communities, poor urban dwellers, AIDS orphans or the disabled, access to education is especially difficult. Four out of five children who do not go to school live in rural regions.

In many countries, traditional role patterns stop parents enrolling girls in school. The stronger the cultural preference for boys in a particular country or region, the greater the gender disparities in the educational sector, for instance in sub-Saharan Africa, the Middle East, and in South and West Asia.

In addition, many children are prevented from going to school on account of crises and wars. The majority of people who are forced to flee armed conflicts are women and children. In many countries where civil war is raging, the majority of schools have been destroyed.

According to Joseph P.G. Chimombo, for more than 40 years, different stakeholders have partnered to support the development of basic education throughout the developing countries. Since independence, the progression achieved in education in developing countries has been remarkable. This massive expansion has been made possible by the infusion of large sums of money by the new governments who saw the expansion of education opportunity as a political necessity. However, while progress has been made notable everywhere including Africa, there are far too many children who do not have a chance to go to school, and far too few who complete the bare minimum of schooling needed to become permanently literate and numerate. This paper discusses the issues surrounding these problems. First, a rationale for education is given before presenting these issues. Then, some of the alternative approaches to the delivery of basic education are outlined and critically discussed while making the case for quality basic education.

Finally, as per Chimombo's experience at the Center for Educational Research and Training (CERT), suggestions for possible areas for research are high lightened. It was at the back of these rationales that African, Asian and Latin American governments expressed their intentions for Universal Primary Education (UPE) in the early 1960s. This movement was rekindled by the recent Jomtein and Dakar Education For All (EFA) conferences. The advocates of UPE contended that mass education will result in an increased supply of educated human power, accelerated economic growth, more social justice, reduced regional disparities, and improved social welfare. At any rate, all children will have an equal start in life regardless of sex, socio-economic background, or geographical location No wonder that as governments strived to reduce poverty and improve the lives of their people, they looked to education as the vehicle for achieving these objectives Article 26 of the 1948 UN universal declaration of human rights said that everyone has a right to education and that this education shall be free and compulsory. It went on to say that education shall be directed to the full development of the human personality and to the strengthening of respect for human rights and fundamental freedoms. If education is viewed as a human right, then EFA implies education for everybody since everybody must have that right.

The challenge towards this drive is how to indeed make education available to all and in good quality. As regard to the purpose of that education, this is all about the role of education in peoples' future's lives. Education has a great significance for the economic social and cultural development. The aim of educational policy should therefore be to give every person a chance of developing his/her inherent potential. It is that kind of education which will bring about inter alia, accelerated economic growth, more wealth and income, decline in population growth, national unity and political stability. In contemporary societies, educational attainment is directly valued and is the main factor leading to advantage of all other key dimensions of individual stratification. Although developing countries experienced massive growth in enrollment soon after independence, such exponential growth has been accompanied by manifold challenges and dilemmas. This section discusses some of the issues surrounding the challenges and dilemmas to the initiatives at getting everybody in school and provide them with quality basic education.

Inadequate Budgets

In most developing countries, the budgets allocated for primary education are too low to meet requirements and to achieve the goal of universal compulsory school attendance. According to the United Nations Educational, Scientific and Cultural Organization (UNESCO), developing countries spend an average of 4.4 per cent of their national income on education. The United States and countries in western Europe invest 5.5 per cent on average, some countries even invest more than 8 per cent on education. In the period between 1999 and 2006, 40 countries reduced their education expenditure—and that figure does not even include many countries that did not supply statistics.

If the primary school system is to keep pace with the growth in the number of school-age children, which is still strong, considerably more money will have to be invested—and the least developed countries (LDCs) at any rate do not have the necessary resources at their disposal. Bad governance, high staff turnover, inefficient use of funding, corruption and lack of management and organisational skills are other obstacles to the universal provision of education.

Lack of Schools and Teaching Staff

Rural regions in particular but also poor urban districts often lack a comprehensive primary school network. Children in rural regions often have to walk extremely long distances to school. Many girls are not allowed to attend schools some distance away as parents are concerned about their safety.

Many schools are poorly equipped. They lack textbooks and

teaching materials, and when these are available, they are often as outdated as the furnishings. Many schools have no funding to cover overheads such as water, electricity or transport for pupils.

Teachers' working conditions are unacceptable in many developing countries: many teachers have to teach two or three shifts a day—in classes with very high student numbers and on poor pay. Many teachers are also poorly trained and ill-prepared for what awaits them in schools. Many countries in sub-Saharan Africa also face a health problem: in some regions so many teachers have contracted AIDS that schools are forced to remain closed.

Many developing countries face the problem of low-quality teaching. The curricula are overloaded with subjects and do not meet the learning needs of the children, and convey distorted or stereotypical images of female and male social role models. Too little account is taken of cultural and regional factors. Teaching times and curricula are too little geared to the children's actual day-to-day reality. Group work, independent learning, critical thought and problem-solving, the use of new technologies and the promotion of life skills are not sufficiently promoted.

Costs of Attending School

Many people in developing countries cannot afford to pay school fees or for learning materials, school uniforms and transport to school. In countries in which school fees have been abolished enrolment rates have risen markedly.

Numerous families rely on the income their children contribute. According to estimates done by the International Labour Organization (ILO), some 166 million children between the ages of 5 and 14 years have to work—often up to 16 hours a day. One in four children in sub-Saharan Africa and one in five children in Asia have to work.

High Illiteracy Rates

Based on estimates, the lack of access to, and often poor quality of, the education systems in developing countries means that some 30 to 50 per cent of those who leave school after four to six years of primary education are neither literate nor numerate. Around 11 per cent of young people between the ages of 15 and 24 are classed as illiterate. Worldwide, around 776 million adults and young people over the age of 15 cannot read or write—just under two thirds of them women.

Between 1970 and 2006, illiteracy rates dropped from 37 to 16 per cent worldwide, but on account of population growth the absolute number of those who cannot read or write has continued to rise in many regions. Ninety-eight per cent of those who cannot read or write live in developing countries.

Sustainable economic development is not possible without qualified experts. But most developing countries lack well-trained specialists. Many countries only have a rudimentary vocational training system, or one that is not integrated into the education and employment system. The courses are usually too theoretical and not geared to the needs of the labour market.

Universities and colleges in developing countries are poorly equipped and lack the necessary funding. Only few are able to sufficiently fulfil their research and teaching responsibilities. However, universities and colleges are important for the entire educational system, when it comes to training specialists and managers, and for tackling development-related tasks at private-sector, government and social level.

Equity and Gender Issues

Another problem in the provision of basic education has been to reach deprived groups. It has become clear that a simple linear expansion of conventional primary schooling faces serious limitations that are due, in the first instance, to the fragility of the demand among the deprived groups in society (Ahmed & Carron 1989). In deprived areas, creating schools does not guarantee that children will attend them. Ahmed and Carron argued that measures to increase the physical accessibility to primary schools and to improve their quality will have to be supplemented by other types of action aimed at stimulating the demand for education while at the same time adapting educational services to the specific needs of deprived local communities. Burney and Irfan (1991) also pointed out that male and female differentials in literacy and school enrolment cannot be attributed to the availability of the schools since enrolment differentials are also influenced by the parental characteristics and socio-economic status of the household.

When educational policies are generally devised to affect the total education system, evidence in Anderson (1988) indicated that certain groups in virtually all societies are disadvantaged in terms of both access to education and opportunity to complete the various levels of education. In some cases, disadvantage is due to insufficient resources and in others, differential impact is as a result of educational policies that are embedded in the social/economic/ political relationship and interactions in the society.

Gender differences are particularly acute when desegregated by urban-rural residence.

Cultural and Religious Attitudes

Culturally determined ways of defining women and men and their roles in a given society shape gender-specific opportunities and constraints. Thus, the existence of discriminatory attitudes towards the schooling of girls is informed by customs and culture. Mobility restrictions arise in many societies when girls reach puberty and this makes the effect to be more on girls' retention than on entry. In some tribes in Africa, as soon as a girl reaches puberty, she is taught the wisdom and knowledge of her society in order to maintain and develop it. These instructions are considered directly relevant to a girl, preparing her for life as a wife and mother in a village. 'Sometimes conflict arises between what is taught at home (in initiation ceremonies) and at school which may lead to parents opposing girls' continued attendance at school'. Indeed, girls' behaviour is often directly related to the many tribal and traditional taboos which dictate what and what not to do at the various stages of their development which may conflict with the demands of schooling. As Davison and Kanyuka (1990) observed, cultural factors in Malawi and gender-specific attitudes about the division of labour also shape the decisions about whether a child should or should not be in school. Another factor which also acts together with attitude is religion. Religious privileges of access have often been restricted to certain classes and to males and this pattern of transmitting and gaining of religious knowledge and power has been influential in determining access and exclusion to formal public education.

Efficiency and Quality

Repeaters cause overcrowding which raises school costs. Clearly, repetition is the key for improving overall efficiency and reaching suitable levels of equity. Davico (1992) found that poor teachers and inadequate support to poor children were to blame for increased rates of repetition and dropout in Brazil. And Patrinos and Psacharopoulos (1996) reported that repetition is especially severe amongst the most deprived, that is those, whose parents have the lowest levels of education and income. Heyneman and Jamison (1980) found that in Uganda, improving the teachers' language ability, the availability of textbooks, school physical facilities, and the pupil's level of health and nutrition were powerful determinants of school achievement. In their study, Kunje and Stuart (1996) indicated that the low quality of education in Malawi schools contributed to the repetition and dropout problem.

REFERENCES

Ashby, J. A. (1985). Equity and Discrimination among Children: Schooling Decisions in Rural Nepal. *Comparative Education Review*, 29 (1), 68-79.

Brock-Utne, B. (2000). *Whose Education for All? The Recolonization of the African Mind*. New York: Falmer Press.

Bryant, C. (1990). *Investigating in People: World Bank Lending for Human Resource Development in Malawi*. Washington DC.

Burney, N. A. & Irfan, M. (1991). Parental Characteristics, Supply of Schools and Child-School Enrolment in Pakistan. *The Pakistan Development Review*, 30 (1), 21-62.

Chimombo, J. P. G. & Kadzamira E. (2001). *Community Participation in Education*. Zomba: CERT.

Chimombo, J. P. G. (2004). *Financing Free Primary Education: Tracing the Self-help Spirit in Malawi*. Paper presented at Hiroshima University, Center for the Study of International Cooperation in Education, Hiroshima, Japan.

Chimombo, J. P. G., Kunje, D. & Chimuzu, T. (2004). *SACMEQ II Report*. Zomba: CERT.

Colclough, C. with Lewin, K. M. (1993). *Educating All the Children: Strategies for Primary Schooling in the South*. Oxford: Clarendon Press.

Dall, F. (1989). *Confronting the Basic Education Crisis: The Zambian Dilemma*. Cambridge: Bridge Project, Harvard University.

Davison, J. & Kanyuka, M. (1990). *An Ethnographic Study of Factors Affecting the Education of Girls in Southern Malawi*. Zomba: Chancellor College. Issues in Basic Education in Developing Countries. An Exploration of Policy Options for Improved Delivery

http://www.answers.com/topic/elementary-education-current-trends#ixzz22mchWnqZ

3
Elementary Education in Asia

Elementary education is the first stage of compulsory education. It is preceded by pre-school or nursery education and is followed by secondary education. In North America, this stage of education is generally followed by middle school. In most countries, it is compulsory for children to receive primary education although it is permissible for parents to provide it. The major goals of primary education are achieving basic literacy and numeracy among all pupils, as well as establishing foundations in science, mathematics, geography, history and other social sciences.

The relative priority of various areas, and the methods used to teach them, are an area of considerable political debate. Typically, primary education is provided in schools, where the child will stay in steadily advancing classes until they complete it and move on to high school/secondary school. Children are usually placed in classes with one teacher who will be primarily responsible for their education and welfare for that year. This teacher may be assisted to varying degrees by specialist teachers in certain subject area often music or physical education.

The continuity with a single teacher and the opportunity to build up a close relationship with the class is a notable feature of the primary education system. Traditionally, various forms of corporal punishment have been an integral part of early education. Recently this practice has come under scrutiny, and in many cases been outlawed, especially in Western countries. In this chapter an overview of primary education of different countries are dealt with. Primary education of different countries, on continental basis is presented in the following chapters. The present chapter deals with elementary education in certain Asian countries.

AFGHANISTAN

In Afghanistan, during the government of the Peoples' Democratic party of Afghanistan reformed the education system; education was stressed for both sexes, and widespread literacy programmes were set up. By 1988, women made up 40 per cent of the doctors and 60 per cent of the teachers at Kabul University which indicates a drastic change. In 1996 the Taliban regime restricted education for females, and the Madrassa became the main source of primary and secondary education. About 1.2 million students were enrolled in schools during the Taliban, with less than 50,000 of them girls.

In 2001, after the overthrow of the Taliban the Karzai administration received substantial international aid to restore the education system. Around 7,000 schools were operating in 20 of the 34 provinces by the end of 2003, with 27,000 teachers teaching 4.2 million children (including 1.2 million girls). Of that number, about 3.9 million were in primary schools. An estimated 57 per cent of men and 86 per cent of women were reported to be illiterate, and the lack of skilled and educated workers was a major economic disadvantage.

The education sector is improved gradually since 2002 and Afghanistan went through a nationwide rebuilding process, and despite some setbacks due to the Taliban insurgency . New educational institutions were established all across the country and more students being enrolled. By 2011 there were 8.2 million students were attending schools in Afghanistan, a country which has about 26 million people living in it.

Girls Education

For Afghani girls, the obstacles to education were even more numerous for Afghan girls. In 2007 that 60 per cent of students were studying in tents or other unprotected structures, and some parents refused to let their daughters attend schools in such conditions. A lack of women teachers was another issue that concerned some parents, especially in more conservative areas. Some parents were not allowing their daughters to be taught by men. But this often meant that girls were not allowed to attend school. In 2009, another concern was the destruction of schools by the Taliban, especially schools for females.

Education in Afghanistan includes K-12 and Higher education, which is supervised by the Ministry of Education and Ministry of Higher Education in Kabul, Afghanistan. According to the Human Development Index, Afghanistan is the 15th least developed country in the world. This is due to decades of war and abandonment by the international community, but on the positive note the country is being carefully rebuilt.

The following achievements were made the last decade:

- Between 2001 and 2010, primary school enrolment rose from around 1 million to nearly 7 million
- The number of teachers in general education has risen sevenfold, but their qualifications are low. About 31 per cent are women.
- Since 2003, over 5,000 school buildings have been rehabilitated or newly constructed. Just over 50 per cent of schools have usable buildings.

In 2010, the United States began establishing a number of Lincoln learning centers in Afghanistan. They are set up to serve as programming platforms offering English language classes, library facilities, programming venues, Internet connectivity, educational and other counseling services. A goal of the programme is to reach at least 4,000 Afghan citizens per month per location.

In June 2011, officials from the United States signed a joint statement with Education minister to expand future opportunities for direct financial support from USAID to the Afghan Ministry of Education.

Afghanistan is one of the worst affected countries by violence against schools, with 670 incidents of attacks on education in 2008. Violence on students have prevented close to 5 million afghan children from attending school in year 2010. In terms of death rates, Afghanistan had 439 teachers, education employees and students killed in 2006-9, one of the highest in the world.

Since the toppling of the Taliban regime, under the combined efforts of Afghan and international experts, the curriculum has been changed from extremist Islamic teachings to one relatively better with new books, and better training. Yet, there still remains no standard curriculum for secondary school textbooks and high school textbooks remain woefully inadequate in number and content.

Infrastructure

In 2012, there were insufficient schools. Around 4,500 schools are being built according to a recent government report. 40 per cent of schools were running in permanent buildings. The rest held classes in the UNICEF shelters or were "desert schools" with students and teachers gathering in the desert near a village.

As a result of the Soviet war, and the civil war which occurred shortly afterwards, many schools were destroyed and the education process as a whole in Afghanistan was negatively affected. The destruction of the education infrastructure went to an extreme level when the Taliban conquered and ruled most of Afghanistan.

Except for some religious education, girls and women were forbidden to learn. Even for men, the curriculum was highly dominated by religious studies instead of science, technology, literature, etc. What the Taliban did in terms of education goes against Islam and what the prophet of Islam, Muhammad, preached. Muhammad told his followers in the early days of Islam to "seek knowledge from the cradle to the grave", and that "the ink of the scholar is more sacred than the blood of the martyr" Islam requires education for all, both men and women.

A lot more still needs to be done in order for Afghanistan to have what modern nations have for their citizens today. An estimated 11 million Afghans are still illiterate , many schools lack proper facilities, the number of qualified teachers are still low, and a major obstacle that needs to be overcome is a cultural bias that many Afghans have, especially in the conservative areas towards the necessity of educating women.

CHINA

As per the educational system existing in People's republic of Chins, all citizens must attend school for at least nine years. The government provides Primary education for six to nine years, starting at age six or seven, followed by six years of secondary education for ages 12 to 18. Some provinces may have five years of primary school but four years for middle school. There are three years of middle school and three years of high school. In 1985, the government abolished tax-funded higher education requiring university applicants to compete for scholarships based on academic ability. In the early 1980s the government allowed the establishment of the private schools.

Primary Education

Primary education includes pre-school education and elementary education. Pre-school, or kindergarten, can last up to three years, with children entering as early as age three, until age six, when they typically enter elementary school. Elementary school begins with the first grade, and then proceeds through either grades five or six, depending on the system. In China, elementary education includes pre-school education, nine-year compulsory education of elementary and junior high schools, regular senior high school education, special education for handicapped children, and elimination of illiteracy.

Central Government has given priority to the development of elementary education, regarding it a key field of development of infrastructure construction and education. Reforms involving the basic issues of elementary education such as increasing government financial input, experimental reform of courses and implementation of a new education appraisal system, are under way in various areas in China.

The Ministry of Finance has allotted five billion yuan from 2001 to 2005 for improving elementary education in poverty-stricken areas, to solve the uneven development of elementary education in different areas and the shortage of funds for compulsory education in rural areas. According to the requirement of the government, the target of reform and development of China's elementary education was to raise the general level of elementary education to or close to that of a moderately developed country by 2010.

Secondary Education

Secondary education is divided into regular secondary education and vocational and technical secondary education. Regular secondary education consists of junior middle school and senior middle school. Junior middle school will involve either three or four years of schooling, depending on the system (6-3 versus 5-4), and senior middle school

Students in the vocational and technical secondary education stream will, upon graduation from junior middle school, enter a vocational or technical school. Vocational schools generally offer programmes ranging from two to four years, and train medium-level skilled workers, farmers, as well as managerial and technical personnel. Technical schools typically offer four year programmes to train intermediate technical personnel. There is a third category, called Schools for Skilled Workers, that typically enroll graduates from junior middle schools to train for positions involving production and operation skills. The length of training is typically three years.

PAKISTAN

In the Constitution of Pakistan, Article 25-A obligates the state to provide free and compulsory quality education to children of age group 5 to 16 years. The school education system in Pakistan is generally divided into four levels: Primary, middle, high and higher secondary schools.

Primary Education

Only 80 per cent of Pakistani children finish primary school education. The standard national system of education is mainly inspired from the pre school in the British system. Pre-school education is designed for 3–5 years old and usually consists of three stages: Play Group, Nursery and Kindergarten (also called 'KG' or 'Prep'). After pre-school education, students go through junior school from grades 1 to 5. This is proceeded by middle school from grades 6 to 8. At middle school, single sex education is usually preferred by the community but co-education is also common in urban cities. The curriculum is usually subject to the institution. The language of instruction depends on the nature of the institution itself, whether it is an English-medium school or an Urdu-medium school.

Pakistan's poor performance in the education sector is mainly caused by the low level of public investment. Public expenditure on education has been 2.2 per cent of GNP in recent years, a marginal increase from 2 per cent before 1984-85. In addition, the allocation of government funds is skewed towards higher education, allowing the upper income class to reap majority of the benefits of public subsidy on education. Lower education institutes such as primary schools suffer under such conditions as the lower income classes are unable to enjoy subsidies and quality education.

There is great difference in the rates of enrollment of boys, as compared to girls in Pakistan. According to UNESCO figures, primary school enrolment for girls stand at 60 per cent as compared to 84 per cent for boys. The secondary school enrolment rate stands at a lower rate of 32 per cent for females and 46 per cent males.

Secondary Education

Secondary education in Pakistan begins from grade 9 and lasts for four years. After end of each of the four school years, students are required to pass a national examination administered by a regional Board of Intermediate and Secondary Education (or BISE).

Upon completion of grade 9, students are expected to take a standardised test in each of the first parts of their academic subjects. They again give these tests of the second parts of the same courses at the end of grade 10. Upon successful completion of these two examinations, they are awarded a Secondary School certificate. This locally termed as 'matriculation certificate' or 'matric' for short. The curriculum usually includes a combination of eight courses including electives (such as Biology, Chemistry, Computing and Physics) as well as compulsory subjects (such as Mathematics, English, Urdu, Islamiyat and Pakistani Studies).

Students then enter an intermediate college and complete grades 11 and 12. Upon completion of each of the two grades, they again take standardised tests in their academic subjects.

SRI LANKA

Constitution of Sri Lanka provide for education as a fundamental right. Sri Lanka's population has a literacy rate of 92 per cent, higher than that expected for a third world country; it has the highest literacy rate in South Asia and overall, one of the highest literacy rates in Asia. Education plays a major part in the life and culture of the country.

Education in Sri Lanka has a history of over 2300 years, it is believed that the Sanskrit language was brought to the island from North India as a result of the establishment of the Budhism. Since then an education system evolved based around the Buddhist temples and monastic colleges, the later primarily intended for the education of clergy and higher education.

With the out set of the expansion in the island, first in the coastal provinces and then interior, Christian missionary societies become active in the field of education. Modern education system was brought about with the integration of Sri Lanka in to the British Empire in the 19th century and it falls under the control of both the Central Government and the Provincial Councils, with some responsibilities lying with the Central Government and the Provincial Council having autonomy for others.

Schools

Lanka derives from the British educational system, which was introduced by the British colonial masters in the 19th century. The British colonial government established colleges for boys and girls separately. These colleges consisted of Primary Schools, Lower Secondary and Higher Secondary schools. Many government schools called Maha Vidyalayas and were started in all parts of the country. The medium of education of Maha Vidyalaya's was either Sinhala or Tamil.

A standard system of schools were begun by the British based on the recommendations of the Colebrooke commission in 1836, this is regarded as the beginning of the modern schooling system in the island. In 1938 the education system in Ceylon (now Sri Lanka) was made free following the granting of Universal franchise in 1931.

In 1942 a special committee was appointed to observe the education system and among the suggestions that followed, the following still play an important role:

(i) Make available to all children a good education free of charge, so that education ceases to be a commodity purchasable only by the urban affluent.

(ii) Make national languages the media of instruction in place of English so that opportunities for higher education, lucrative employment open only to small number of the urban affluent, would become available to others as well.
(iii) Rationalize the school system so that educational provision is adequate, efficient and economical.
(iv) Ensure that every child is provided with instruction in the religion of his/her parents.
(v) Protect teachers from exploitation by managers of schools.
(vi) Make adequate provision for adult education.

After independence, the number of schools and the literacy rate of the people substantially increased. Many schools were built in the post colonial era. However, the established schools who had their origins in the colonial era dominate social life in Sri Lanka mainly due the network of old boys and old girls.

Several superficial changers to the school system took place in the post independence era by successive governments, these include the change of the primary medium of education to the national languages, nationalization of private schools and the introduction of national/provisional school system.

Primary and Secondary Education

Today primary education lasts six years, after which the pupils sit a scholarship examination. Those who passed scholarship examination are qualify themselves to be admitted to popular schools and are granted monthly financial support until they pass out from the university.

After primary education there is Junior Secondary education which lasts for five years, after which pupils have to sit government examination namely G.C.E. ordinary level to qualify for Senior Secondary education which last another two years. Then comes the competitive university entrance examination which is called G.C.E. Advanced level examination.

Those who are not admitted to the universities can either enter vocational technical schools or be employed in companies or in government departments as apprentice or trainees. They can also pursue higher education as external students of traditional universities or at the Open university of Sri Lanka. Medium of study in schools today is either Sinhala or Tamil depending on the native language. The first language and the mathematics are compulsory subjects. All primary junior secondary pupils get their schools uniforms and text books free of charge from the government.

Sri Lanka's education structure is divided into five parts: primary, junior secondary, senior secondary, collegiate and tertiary. Primary education lasts five to six years (Grades 1-5) and at the end of this period, the students may elect to write a national exam called the Scholarship exam. This exam allows students with exceptional skills to move on to better schools. After primary education, the junior secondary level lasts for 4 years (Grades 6-9) followed by 2 years (Grades 10-11) of the senior secondary level. According to the Sri Lankan law, it is compulsory that all children go to school till grade 9 (age 14) at which point they can choose to continue their education or drop out and engage in apprenticeship for a job or farming

UNITED ARAB EMIRATES

The United Arab Emirates currently devotes approximately 25 per cent of total federal government spending to education. The overall literacy rate is 91 per cent. The development of education in the UAE started effectively in 1962, where the number of schools then was barely 20 schools, in which less than 4000 students studied, mostly male students. The necessary infrastructure was often unavailable in many social services venues including hospitals, households, airports etc. due to the lack of necessary manpower.

Provision of quality education in the United Arab Emirates began shortly after the establishment of the federation with the inception of the first university in Al Ain, Abu Dhabi, the United Arab Emirates University. Since then, the country has progressed with efforts of ensuring high literacy rates, modern programmes and women's share in education.

Upon the exploration of Oil and the beginning of development, the UAE focused a lot of attention on education, as His Highness Sheikh Zayed Bin Sultan Al Nahyan considered education among the priorities of progress. He said openly that the Youth are the real wealth of the Nation. He was overly generous when it came to education related projects that aspired for the gradual improvement of education in order to prepare a new generation capable of contributing to the progress of the Nation.

When the Federation was established in 1971, educational services were still immature and inaccessible to many cities and villages. Enrollment rate was nearly 28 thousand students. Higher education was unavailable locally; therefore students had to seek other countries to pursue higher education after school on the government expense. At the same time, the state leadership sought tirelessly to prepare the necessary infrastructure for the educational sector.

Government educational institutions supervising education were established in 1970, whereas regular education was organized to be in four stages:

- Kindergarten (4-5 years)
- Elementary (6-11 years)
- Intermediate (12-14 years)
- Secondary (15-17 years)

Accordingly, education witnessed a development process run by the government in which all necessary tools were provided. It included both male and female students alike, to get their free public schooling. At a later stage, private education appeared to complement public education to provide schooling for almost 40 per cent of UAE students.

Private education distinguished itself with a special attention given to the education of foreign languages for national and expatriate students, in addition to other subjects like science and math. Education continued to be an obsession for the State, which lead to the adoption of a futuristic plan for the development of education during the next twenty years, with a vision polarized on reaching higher standards in line with the inputs of science and technology. The plan incorporates the education of information technology, eradication of computer illiteracy, preserving social values and ethics, and promoting traditional values among the youth

Women and Education

UAE women utilized to the maximum all opportunities provided through the various educational programmes run by the government, and they proved to be highly responsible. The high schools results for three consecutive years (1996-1999) were a real evidence of women excellence, since the highest grades and best results were recorded for female students; a factor that lead many UAE women to occupy leadership positions on different governmental levels.

Women work side by side with men in both the public and private sectors, and proved themselves through excellence that compares to men working in similar positions. Currently, the female graduates of Al Ain University and Technology colleges are working in different companies and administrations, where they perform many duties and careers including Engineering, Applied Sciences, Media.

Basic Education

Public education is free for male and female citizen children through the university level. Beginning in the academic year 2006-07, *expatriate* students may, for a fee, attend government schools. The UAE has one of the lowest student-to-teacher ratios (15:1) in the world.

Despite not being among the highest rated on the Education Index, the UAE has made regionally significant achievements in ensuring women's access to education. UNDP's Millennium Development Goal No. 3, to "Promote Gender Equality and Empower Women" has reached its targeted levels of female participation in primary education and continues to increase.

IRAN

In Iran, there are both free public schools and private schools at all levels, from elementary school through university. Education in Iran is highly centralized. The Ministry of Education is in charge of educational planning, financing, administration, curriculum, and textbook development. Teacher training, grading, and examinations are also the responsibility of the Ministry. At the university level, however, every student attending public schools is required to commit to serve the government for a number of years typically equivalent to those spent at the university, or pay it off for a very low price (typically a few hundred dollars). During the early 1970s, efforts were made to improve the educational system by updating school curriculum introducing modern textbooks, and training more efficient teachers.

Primary school starts at the age of 6 for a duration of 5 years. Middle school, also known as orientation cycle, goes from the sixth to the eighth grade. High School , for which the last three years is not mandatory, is divided between theoretical, vocational/technical and manual, each programme with its own specialties.

Modern Education

Khomeini's regime put its own stamp on the process of education. The most important change was the 'Islamization' of the education system. All students were segregated by sex. In 1980, the Cultural Revolution Committee was formed to oversee the institution of Islamic values in education. Teaching materials based on Islam were introduced into the primary grades within six months of the revolution.

Upgrading the quality of the educational system at all levels, as well as reforming education curricula, was envisaged by the Fourth Five year development plan (2005-10).

Women in Education

Women make up more than 60 per cent of Iranian university students with some fields in science and engineering having more than 70 per cent of their alumni be women. According to UNESCO world survey, Iran has the highest female to male ratio at primary level of enrollment in the world among sovereign nations, with a girl to boy ratio of 1.22 : 1.00.

INDONESIA

The Dutch introduced a system of formal education for the local population of Indonesia, although this was restricted to certain privileged children Elementary education was introduced by the Dutch in Indonesia during the colonial era. Initially, it was reserved for the Dutch and other Europeans only.

The system they introduced was roughly similar to the current structure, with the following levels indicated in its Dutch name:

- **ELS** (Europeesche Lagere School)—Primary School for Europeans
- **HIS** (Hollandsch-Inlandsche School)—Primary School for Natives
- **MULO** (Meer Uitgebreid Lager Onderwijs)—Middle School
- **AMS** (Algeme(e)ne Middelbare School)—High School or College
- **HBS** (Hogere Burger School)—Pre-University

The segregation between Dutch and Indonesian in Education pushed several Indonesian figures to start educational institutions for local people. Pesantrens were also mushrooming rapidly during this time period. Education in Indonesia is under the responsibility of the Ministry of Education and Culture and the Ministry of Religious Affairs. In Indonesia, all citizens must undertake nine years of compulsory education which consists of six years at elementary level and three in secondary level. Islamic schools are under the responsibility of the Ministry of Religious Affairs.

Education is defined as a planned effort to establish a study environment and education process so that the student may actively develop his/her own potential to gain the religious and spiritual level, consciousness, personality, intelligence, behavior and creativity to him/herself, other citizens and for the nation. The Constitution also notes that education in Indonesia is divided into two major parts, formal and non-formal. Formal education is further divided into three levels, primary, secondary and tertiary education.

Schools in Indonesia are run either by the government or private sectors. Some private schools refer to themselves as "national plus schools" which means that they intend to go beyond the minimum government requirements, especially with the use of English as medium of instruction or having an international-based curriculum instead of the national one.

Era of Islamic States

The emergence of Islamic state in Indonesia is noted by the acculturation of both Islamic tradition and Hindu-Buddhist tradition. At this time period, "Pondok pesantren", a type of Islamic boarding school was introduced and several of them were established. The location of pesantren is mostly far away from the hustling crowd of the city, resembling the location of Karsyan.

Early Education

From the age of 2, some children in Indonesia attend pre school play group From the age of 4, they attend kindergarten. This education is not compulsory for Indonesian citizens, as it is aimed to prepare them for Primary Schooling. The kindergarten years are usually divided into "Class A" and "Class B" students spending a year in each class.

Primary School

Children aged 6–11 attend Primary School. The primary level is compulsory for all Indonesian citizens, according to the Constitution. In contrast to the majority of privately run kindergartens, most elementary schools are government-operated public schools. Similar to education systems in the U.S., students must spend six years to complete this level. Some schools offer an accelerated learning programme, where students who perform well can complete the level in five years.

Middle School

Middle School, abbreviated as "SMP" (Sekolah Menengah Pertama) is part of basic education in Indonesia. After graduating from primary school, students attend Middle School for three years from the age of 12 to 14. After three years of schooling and graduation, students may move on to High School.

High School

There are two types of High Schools in Indonesia. The first is generally known 'Sekolah Menengah Ata' and second is 'Sekolah Menengah Kejuruan'. SMA differs from SMK in their studies. The students at SMA are prepared to continue their study to university while students of SMK are prepared to be ready to work after graduation, even sans university education. Students attending SMA will be divided into three group of studies in their 11th grade, i.e. Science, Social studies, and Linguistics. According to the Constitution, this level of education is not compulsory.

ISRAEL

According to the Organization for Economic Cooperation and Development's Education at a Glance report, released in 2012, Israel was named the second most educated country in the world. The report found that 78 per cent of the money invested in education is from public funds and 45 per cent of the population has a university or college diploma.

Israeli schools are divided into four tracks: state (*Mamlachti*), state-religious (*Mamlachti dati*), Independent (*Haredi*) schools (*Chinuch Atzmai*) and Arab. There are also private schools which reflect the philosophies of specific groups of parents (Democratic Schools) or that are based on the curriculum of a foreign country (e.g. The American International School in Israel). The majority of Israeli children attend state schools.

Education in Israel refers to the comprehensive education system of Israel. Expenditure on education accounts for approximately 10 per cent of GDP, and most schools are subsidized by the state. The education system consists of three tiers: primary education (grades 1-6, approx. ages 6–12), middle school (grades 7-9, approx. ages 12–15) and high school (grades 10-12, approx. ages 15–18). Compulsory education takes place from kindergarten through to 12th grade.

The proportions of pupils attending schools in the Haredi and Arab sectors are increasing; according to a demographic study published in 2009, Haredim and Arabs together will amount to 60 per cent of Israel's elementary school population by 2030.

The Israeli Pupils' Rights Law of 2000 prohibits discrimination of students for sectarian reasons in admission to or expulsion from an educational institution, in establishment of separate educational curricula or holding of separate classes in the same educational institution, and addresses rights and obligations of pupils.

JAPAN

In Japan, more than 99 per cent of elementary school-age children are enrolled in school. All children enter first grade at age six, and starting school is considered a very important event in a child's life. Virtually all elementary education takes place in public schools; less than 1 per cent of the schools are private. Private school tended to be costly, although the rate of cost increases in tuition for these schools had slowed in the 1980s. Some private elementary schools are prestigious, and they serve as a first step to higher-level private schools with which they are affiliated, and thence to a University. Competition to enter some of these "ladder schools" is quite intense.

Although public elementary education is free, some school expenses are borne by parents. For many families, there are also nonschool educational expenses, for extra books, or private lessons. Costs for private elementary schools are substantially higher.

Elementary school classes are large, about thirty-one students per class on average, but higher numbers are permitted. Students are usually organized into small work groups, which have both academic and disciplinary functions. Discipline is maintained and a sense of responsibility encouraged, by the use of student monitors and by having the students assume responsibility for the physical appearance of their classroom and school.

Courses of Study

The curriculum includes Japanese language, Social studies, arithmetic and Science. Nonacademic subjects taught include art and handicrafts, music, homemaking, physical education and moral education. Japanese language is an emphasized subject.

The English language is taught at some schools especially in the higher grades; it is now mandatory at 5th and 6th grade from 2011, as in 2002 TOEFL scores in Japan were the worst in Asia after North Korea.

There is a system of educational television and radio, and

almost all elementary schools use programmes prepared by the School Education Division of Japan's ex Broadcasting Corporation. In addition to broadcast media schools increasingly are equipped with computers.

Virtually all elementary schoolchildren receive a full lunch at school. Although subsidized by the government, the programme is not altogether free. Full meals usually consist of bread (or increasingly, of rice), a main dish, and milk. Although the programme grew out of concern in the immediate post-war period for adequate nutrition. Because there are relatively few cafeterias in elementary schools, meals are taken in the classroom with the teacher, providing another informal opportunity for teaching nutrition and health and good eating habits and social behavior. Frequently, students also are responsible for serving the lunch and cleaning up.

Problems

Japanese elementary schooling is seen as comparatively effective, but not without some problems, notably increasing absenteeism and school refusal a troublesome amount of bullying. In addition, special provision for the young children returning to Japan from long periods spent overseas is an issue. The government also is concerned with the education of Japanese children residing abroad. However, in most urban centers there are at least private *international schools* which can accommodate such returnees.

Elementary school education is seen in Japan as fundamental in shaping a positive attitude toward lifelong education. Regardless of academic achievement, almost all children in elementary school are advanced to *junior high schools* (lower secondary schools), the second of the two compulsory levels of education.

RUSSIA

According to the 2002 Census, the literacy rate in Russia is 99.4 per cent (99.7 per cent men, 99.2 per cent women). 16 per cent of population over 15 years of age (17.6 million) have tertiary (undergraduate level or higher) education; 47.7 per cent have completed secondary education (9 or 10 years old); 26.5 per cent have completed middle school (8 or 9 years old) and 8.1 per cent have elementary education (5 years old). Highest rates of tertiary education 24.7 per cent are recorded among women aged 35–39 years (compared to 19.5 per cent for men of the same age bracket).

Education in Russia is provided predominantly by the state and is regulated by the Ministry of education and science. Regional authorities regulate education within their jurisdiction within the prevailing framework of federal laws.

Pre-school Education

Kindergartens, unlike schools, are regulated by regional and local authorities. The ministry of Education and Science regulates only a brief pre-school preparation programme for the 5–6 year old children. In 2004 the government attempted to charge full cost of kindergartens to the parents; widespread public opposition caused a reversal of policy. Currently, local authorities can legally charge the parents not more than 20 per cent of cost. Twins, children of university students, refugees, Chernobyl veterans and other protected social groups are entitled to free service.

The Soviet system provided for nearly universal primary (nursery, age 1 to 3) and kindergarten (age 3 to 7) service in urban areas, relieving working mothers from daytime child care needs. After the collapse of the Soviet Union the number decreased to 46,000; kindergarten buildings were sold as real estate, irreversibly rebuilt and converted for office use.

Secondary School

According to a 2005 UNESCO report, 96 per cent of the adult population has completed lower secondary schooling and most of them also have an upper secondary education Eleven-year secondary education in Russian is compulsory since September 1, 2007. Until 2007, it was limited to nine years with grades 10-11 optional. A student of 15 to 18 years of age *may* drop out of school with approval of his/her parent and local authorities, and without their consent upon reaching age of 18. Expulsion from school for multiple violations disrupting school life is possible starting at the age of 15. The eleven-year school term is split into elementary (grades 1-4), middle (grades 5-9) and senior (grades 10-11) classes. Absolute majority of children attend full programme schools providing eleven-year education; schools limited to elementary or elementary and middle classes typically exist in rural areas.

The school year extends from September 1 to end of May and is divided into four terms. Study programme in schools is fixed; unlike in some Western countries, school children or their parents have no choice of study subjects. Students are graded on a 5-step scale, ranging in practice from 2 ("unacceptable") to 5 ("excellent"); 1 is a rarely used sign of extreme failure. Teachers regularly subdivide these grades (i.e. 4+, 5-) in daily use, but term and year results are graded strictly 2, 3, 4 or 5

Unified State Examinations

Traditionally, the universities and institutes conducted their own admissions tests regardless of the applicants' school record. There were no uniform measure of graduates' abilities; marks issued by high schools were perceived as incompatible due to grading variances between schools and regions. In 2003 the Ministry of Education launched the Unified State Examination programme. The set of standardised tests for high school graduates, issued uniformly throughout the country and rated independent of the student's schoolmasters, akin to North American SAT was supposed to replace entrance exams to state universities.

REFERENCES

Afghanistan's Ministry of Education (MoE) website (http://www.moe.gov.af

Andreeva, L. V. *et al.* (2007). *Education of disabled people in the context of UNESCO EFA programme: experience of Russia.* Saint Petersburg: Herzen University Publishing House. *ISBN 978-5-8064-1149-6.* see also: *Russian version*

Blood, P. (1994). *"Pakistan-Education". Pakistan: A Country Study.* GPO for the Library of Congress.

Historical Overview of Education in Sri Lanka: Ancient Period (543 BC-1500 AD), Ministry of Education.

Historical Overview of Education in Sri Lanka: The British Period: (1796-1948) Ministry of Education.

http://www.cmb.ac.lk/academic/medicine/history.html

http://www.depdiknas.go.id/statistik/thn04-05/SMA_0405.htm

http://www.docstoc.com/docs/17199577/Introduction-to-Pakistan

http://www.justiceministry.gov.lk/

http://www.mohe.gov.sa/en/studyinside/Government-Universities/Pages/default.aspx

http://www.presstv.com/Program/226126.html

http://www.presstv.com/Program/230432.html

http://www.reuters.com/article/2011/01/01/us-afghanistan-education-idUSTRE7000P220110101 Retrieved 10 February 2012

http://www.statpak.gov.pk/depts/fbs/statistics/pslm_prov2006-07/2.14a.pdf

http://www.unesco.org/education/GMR2006/full/chapt7_eng.pdf - Figure 7.7:

https://www.cia.gov/library/publications/the-world-factbook/geos/ae.html

Jason John, N. and Aytng, S. (2011). *The Business Year 2011: Iran*. London, U.K.: The Business Year. p. 232. *ISBN 978-1-908180-00-1.*

Johnson, D. (2010), *Politics, Modernisation and Educational Reform in Russia: From Past to Present* (2010).

Kindergarten statistics between 2004-2005 *http://www.depdiknas.go.id/statistik/thn04-05/TK_0405.htm*

Munir, B. (2004). *Higher Education in the Arab States, Beirut: UNESCO Regional Bureau for Education in the Arab States. Saudi Arabia*

Primary School statistics between 2004-2005 *http://www.depdiknas.go.id/statistik/thn04-05/SD_0405.htm*

This article incorporates public domain material from websites or documents of the Library of Congress Country Studies. - Japan

UNDP Millennium Development Goals United Arab Emirates Report, March 2007 *http://www.undp.org.ae/Upload/Doc/NMDGs-Eng2007.pdf*; pg. 14

UNICEF Country Statistics for the UAE, 2006 *http://www.unicef.org/infobycountry/uae_statistics.html#46*

4

Elementary Education in Europe

Elementary Education is some of the European countries are discussed below:

BELGIUM

Education in Belgium is regulated and for the larger part financed by one of the three communities: Flemish, French and German-speaking. All three communities have a unified school system with small differences from one community to another. The national government plays a very small role: it decides directly the age for mandatory schooling and indirectly the financing of the communities. Education in Belgium is compulsory between the ages of 6 and 18. Private home education is possible, and the numbers are rising slowly.

In the past there were conflicts between state schools and catholic schools, and disputes whether the latter should be funded by the government. The 1958 School Pact was an agreement of the three large political parties to end these conflicts.

Stages of Education

Pre School

Free pre-primary schooling is provided to every child from the age of 2 years 6 months. In most schools the child can start in school as soon as they reach this age, so class size for the youngest children grows during the year. In the Flemish region, start dates are limited to 6 per year, after a school holiday period and the first school day in February.

The aim of pre-school is to develop, in a playful way, children's cognitive skills, their capacity to express themselves and communicate, their creativity and independence. There are no formal lessons or assessments, and everything is done in a playful way.

Although it is not compulsory, more than 90 per cent of all children in the age category attend pre-school. Most pre-schools are attached to a particular primary school. Preschools and primary schools often share buildings and other facilities.

Primary School

Primary school consists of six years and the subjects given are generally the same at all schools. Primary schooling is free and age is the only entrance requirement.

Primary education is divided into three cycles:

- First cycle (year 1 and 2)
- Second cycle (year 3 and 4)
- Third cycle (year 5 and 6)

Education in primary schools is rather traditional: it concentrates on reading, writing and basic mathematics, but also touches already a very broad range of topics (biology, music, religion, history, etc.)

Secondary School

When graduating from primary school around the age of 12, students enter secondary education. Here they have to choose a course that they want to follow, depending on their skill level and interests.

Secondary education consists of three cycles:

- First cycle (year 1 and 2)
- Second cycle (year 3 and 4)
- Third cycle (year 5 and 6)

The Belgian secondary education grants the pupils more choice as they enter a higher cycle. The first cycle provides a broad general basis, with only a few options to choose from (such as Latin, additional mathematics, technology). This should enable students to orient themselves in the most suitable way towards the many different courses available in the second and third stages. The second and third cycle are much more specific in each of the possible directions. While the youngest pupils may choose at the most two or four hours per week, the oldest pupils have the opportunity to choose between different "menus": like Math-Science, Sociology-Languages or Latin-Greek. They are then able to shape the largest part of the time they spend at school. However, some core lessons are compulsory like the first language and sport, etc. This mix between compulsory and optional lessons grouped in menus make it possible to keep class structures even for the oldest students.

DENMARK

Education in Denmark is compulsory for children below the age of 15 or 16, even though it is not compulsory to attend Folkskole ("public school"). The school years up to the age of fifteen/sixteen are known as Folkeskole, since any education has to match the level offered there. About 82 per cent of young people take further education in addition to this. Government-funded education is usually free of charge and open to all. Denmark has a tradition of private schools and about 13 per cent of all children at basic school level attend private schools.

The Danish education system has its origin in the cathedral- and monastery schools established by the Roman Catholic church in the early Middle ages and seven of the schools established in the 12th and 13th centuries still exist today. Popular elementary education was at that time still very primitive, but in 1721, 240 cavalry schools were established throughout the kingdom. The philanthropic thoughts of such people as Roussaeu also helped spur developments in education open to all children.

The Education Index, published with the UN's human development Index in 2008, based on data from 2006, lists Denmark as 0.993, amongst the highest in the world, tied for first with Australia, Finland and New Zealand.

In Denmark, 9 years of primary school (*Folkeskole*) are compulsory.

Kindergarten (optional): 5–6 years

- 0th grade: 5-7 years
- 1st grade: 6–8 years
- 2nd grade: 7–9 years
- 3rd grade: 8-10 years
- 4th grade: 9–11 years
- 5th grade: 10–12 years
- 6th grade: 11–13 years
- 7th grade: 12–14 years
- 8th grade: 13–15 years
- 9th grade: 14–16 years
- 10th grade (optional): 15–18 years

FRANCE

It used to be commonly accepted that the French Education system was one of the best in the world. Today, though any such a bold overall affirmation must be open to question, it is still true to say that the French education system is one of the more successful in the world, and that in certain fields it remains a world leader. According to the OECD, France's education system is average, compared to other developed countries.

Education is compulsory in France from the ages of 6 to 16, but a large majority of children start school well before the minimum age, often as young as two years old, and over 50 per cent of 18-21 year olds in France are still in full-time education, or else following a vocational training course. Some 64 per cent of all school pupils in France complete their secondary education, and take the high-school leaving certificate examinations, known as the baccalauréat or the baccalauréat professionnel.

Types of School

Kindergarten (Ecole Maternelle and Creches);

Kindergarten or pre-school Ecoles Maternelles take pupils from age 2 to age 6, and prepare them for entry into primary school. The French école maternelle is more than just a playschool; the curriculum includes reading and writing, numeracy and even sometimes a foreign language, as well as artistic and creative activities.

Prior to nursery schools, there are also a lot of private and public nurseries, called *crèches*. These daycare centers keep babies from 2 months to 3 years old, until they can attend the Ecole Maternelle. There are several types of crèches providing different services (regular or temporary child care), size (from 10 to 60 children) and management. There are more than 11,000 Crèches in France, but getting a slot can be hard, and mothers are advised to look for a slot as soon as they are pregnant.

Primary School (Ecole primaire, or Ecole élémentaire)

Primary school, grade school. Five classes, ages 6 to 11. The primary school curriculum in France is similar to that in other countries, and includes literacy and numeracy, with classes in French, arithmetic, but also geography and history, the arts, and more and more frequently a foreign language, usually English. Pupils have an average of 28 hours classes per week. The five classes in the Ecole Primaire are, in order, CP (preparatory class), CE1, CE2, (CE means cours élémentaire—elementary class) CM1, and CM2 (CM is cours moyen, middle class); the two middle classes are a preparation for the next level, which is middle school.

High School (Lycée)

High School. The traditional French lycée covers the last three years of secondary education. There are two main types of traditional lycée, the lycée général or lycée classique, and the lycée technique. In big towns and cities, there will be a mix of both types; in smaller towns, there may not be a lycée tehnique. The main function of the lycée is to prepare pupils to sit the baccalaureat exam, the equivalent of British A levels. Classes in a traditional lycée cover the same range as in collège, with the addition of philosophy (for all) in the final year.

Pupils in a lycée technique may begin to specialise in a fairly narrow technical field, in addition to their general secondary studies. There are technical lycées specialising in fields such as microtechnologies or aeronautics. Technical lycées that provide training in very specialised fields are usually boarding schools, since they recruit pupils from a large catchment area, and even on occasions from all over France.

Public and Private Schools in France

It is commonly believed, outside France, that virtually all schools in France are state schools, i.e. in the public sector. This is a misconception. Over 80 per cent of school pupils are in state schools, but this leaves a substantial (and growing) minority of almost 20 per cent who attend private schools—far more, for instance, than in the United Kingdom or the USA.

However the private/public divide is not as clear as it is in other countries. Private schools in France are essentially (about 90 per cent) catholic schools, in which there is religious instruction in the curriculum; they select their own teachers, but must follow the same curriculum as state schools if they wish to remain under contract to the state education system. This is a very important point for almost all private schools, as it means that the state pays the teachers. Consequently, private schools in France only charge symbolic or low fees, and are accessible to pupils from all sectors of society, not just to those whose parents are well-off. There are only a handful of fee-paying boarding schools in France, similar to English "public schools".

The state education system attaches great importance to the principle of secularism and there is no formal teaching of religion in state schools in France. In theory, religion has no place in state schools in France. However, recent events in France have led to a growing demand for schools to teach religious awareness, this being seen by some as necessary for the development of greater understanding between people of different religions, notably with regard to France's Islamic minority. Religious instruction is not banned from state schools in France; it can take place after hours, for pupils who wish.

GERMANY

The responsibility for the German education system lies primarily with the states (*Länder*) while the federal government plays only a minor role. Optional Kindergarten (nursery school) education is provided for all children between three and six years of age, after which school attendance is compulsory, in most cases for 11 to 12 years. The system varies throughout Germany because each state (*Land*) decides its own educational policies. Most children, however, first attend Grundschule from the age of six to ten or twelve.

Historically, Lutheranism had a strong influence on German culture, including its education Martin Luther advocated compulsory schooling so that all people would independently be able to read and interpret the Bible. This concept became a model for schools throughout Germany.

German secondary education includes five types of school. The Gymnasium is designed to prepare pupils for university education and finishes with the final examination Abitur, after grade 12 or 13. The Realschule has a broader range of emphasis for intermediate pupils and finishes with the final examination Mittlere Reife, after grade 10; the Hauptschule prepares pupils for vocational education and finishes with the final examination after grade 9 or 10 and the Realschulabschluss after grade 10.

There are two types of grade 10: one is the higher level called type 10b and the lower level is called type 10a; only the higher level type 10b can lead to the Realschule and this finishes with the final examination after grade 10b. During the one-year qualifying period of the change to the new regulations, pupils could continue with class 10 to fulfill the statutory period of education.

Four different types of secondary schools developed.

- A nine-year classical *Gymnasium* (including study of Latin and Classical Greek or Hebrew, plus one modern language);
- A nine-year *Real gymnasium* (focusing on Latin, modern languages, science and mathematics);
- A six-year *Realschule* (without university entrance qualification, but with the option of becoming a trainee in one of the modern industrial, *office* or technical jobs); and
- A nine-year *Oberrealschule* (focusing on modern languages, science and mathematics).

By the turn of the 20th century, the four types of schools had achieved equal rank and privilege, although they did not have equal prestige.

Teachers are employed by the Ministry of Education for the state and usually have a job for life after a certain period which, however, is not comparable in timeframe nor competitiveness to the typical tenure track. This practice depends on the state and is currently changing. A parents' council is elected to voice the parents' views to the school's administration. Each class elects one or class presidents, if two are elected usually one is male and the other female, the class presidents meet several times a year as the Students' council. A team of school presidents is also elected by the pupils each year, their main purpose is organizing school parties, sports tournaments and the like for their fellow students. The local town is responsible for the school building and employs the janitorial and secretarial staff.

Church and state are separated in Germany. Compulsory school prayers and compulsory attendance at religious services are against the constitution. In 1995, it was ruled that the Christian cross was not allowed in classrooms, as it violates the religious freedom of non-Christian students. The cross is allowed if none of the pupils objects, but must be removed in the event of an objection. Some German states have banned teachers from wearing headscarves.

Pre School

The German preschool is known as a *Kindergarten*. Children between the ages of 3 and 6 attend *Kindergarten* which are not part of the school system. They are often run by city or town administrations, churches, or registered societies, many of which follow a certain educational approach as represented by Montessori or Reggio Emilia.

Kindergärten can be open from 7 a.m. to 5 p.m. or longer and may also house a *Kinderkrippe*, meaning crèche, for children between the ages of eight weeks and three years, and possibly an afternoon *Hort* (often associated with a primary school) for school-age children aged 6 to 10 who spend the time after their lessons there. Alongside nurseries, there are day-care nurses working independently from any pre-school institution in individual homes and looking after only three to five children typically up to three years of age. These nurses are supported and supervised by local authorities.

Primary Education

Parents looking for a suitable school for their child have a wide choice of elementary schools. State schools do not charge tuition fees. The majority of pupils attend state schools in their neighbourhood. Schools in affluent areas tend to be better than those in deprived areas. Once children reach school age, many middle-class and working-class families move away from deprived areas.

Public and Private Schools

In 2006, six per cent of German children attended private schools. In Germany Article 7, Paragraph 4 of the Constitution of Germany, guarantees the right to establish private schools.

Ersatzschulen are ordinary primary or secondary schools which are run by private individuals, private organizations or religious groups. These schools offer the same types of diplomas as in public schools. However, Ersatzschulen lack the freedom to operate completely outside government control. Teachers at Ersatzschulen are required to have at least the same qualifications as those at state schools; by the same token, their salaries are at least those of teachers at state schools. An Ersatzschule must have at least the same academic standards as those of a state school and Article 7, Paragraph 4 of the Constitution, also forbids the segregation of pupils according to the means of their parents. Therefore, most Ersatzschulen have very low tuition fees compared to those in most other western European countries; scholarships are also often available. However, it is not possible to finance these schools with such low tuition fees: accordingly all German Ersatzschulen are subsidised with public funds.

REPUBLIC OF IRELAND

The Constitution of Ireland allows this education to be provided in the home; this has caused much legal wrangling for years as to the minimum standards required for home education since the constitution does not explicitly provide for the State to define these minimum standards.

The levels of education in Ireland are primary, secondary and higher (often known as "third-level") education. In recent years further education has grown immensely. Growth in the economy since the 1960s has driven much of the change in the education system. Education in Ireland is free at all levels, including college (university), but only for students applying from the European Union.

English is the primary medium of instruction at all levels, except in Galescoileanna i.e., schools in which Irish is the working language and which are increasingly popular. Universities also offer degree programmes in diverse disciplines, taught mostly through English, with a few in Irish. Some universities also offer some courses partly through other languages such as French, German or Spanish.

Education is compulsory for all children in Ireland from the ages of six to 16 or until students have completed three years of second level education and including one sitting of the Junior Certificate examination although it is most common to start primary education aged four or five.

Children are typically enrolled in the Junior Infant class at the age of either four or five depending on the wishes of their parents and the policy of the school. Some schools require the child to have attained the age of four before a specific date in order to enroll. Otherwise, the child must seek a place in a different school or wait until the next year to enroll.

Pre-school

Pre-school is optional in Ireland and takes the form of a number of privately run crèches, play-schools and Montessori schools, which children attend for one year or two, at ages three and/or four. Parents must pay to send their child to these institutions using their own earnings and any child allowance they receive from the government.

Primary Education

The Primary School Curriculum is prepared by the National Council for Curriculum and Assessment and is perhaps unusual in leaving to church authorities the formulation and implementation of the religious curriculum in the schools they control.

The Primary Certificate Examination (1929–1967) was the terminal examination at this level until the first primary-school curriculum, The primary school system consists of eight years: Junior and Senior Infants (corresponding to Kindergarten), and First to Sixth Classes. Most children attend primary school between the ages of 4 and 12 although it is not compulsory until the age of 6. A minority of children start school at 3.

National schools date back to the introduction of state primary education in 1831. They are usually controlled by a board of management under diocesan patronage and often include a local clergyman. The term "national school" has of late become partly synonymous with primary school in some parts.

Secondary Education

Most students attend and complete secondary education, with approximately 90 per cent of school-leavers taking the terminal examination, the Leaving Certificate, at age 16–19. Secondary education is generally completed at one of four types of school.

Secondary schools, are owned and managed by religious communities or private organisations. Vocational schools are owned and managed by Vocational Education Committees.

In urban areas, there is considerable freedom in choosing the type of school the child will attend. The emphasis of the education system at second level is as much on breadth as on depth; the system attempts to prepare the individual for society and further education or work. This is similar to the education system in Scotland

Therefore, a typical secondary school will consist of First to Third Year (with the Junior Certificate at the end of Third), the usually optional Transition Year (though compulsory in some schools), and Fifth and Sixth Year (with the Leaving Certificate at the end of Sixth).

NORWAY

Education in Norway is mandatory for all children aged 6–16. Norway introduced the *folkeskole*, a primary school which became mandatory for 7 years in 1889 and 9 years in 1969. In the 1970s and 1980s, the *folkeskole* was abolished, and the *grunnskole* was introduced.

Today the Norwegian school system can be divided into three parts: Elementary school (*Barneskole*, age 6-13), lower secondary school (*Ungdomsskole*, age 13-16), and upper secondary school (*Videregående skole*, age 16-19).

Primary School (*Barneskole*, grades 1–7, age 6–13)

In the first year of primary school, the students are mostly playing educational games, learning social structures, learning the alphabet, basic addition and subtraction, and basic English skills. In grades 2 through 7 (years 3–8), they are introduced to Mathematics, English, Norwegian, Science, Religion, Aesthetics, and Gymnastics. No official grades are given at this level, however, the teacher often writes a comment—analysis and sometimes an unofficial grade on tests. Tests are to be taken home and shown to parents. They also have an introductory test to let teacher know if the student is above the grade average or is in need of some assistance at school.

Lower Secondary School (*Ungdomsskole*, grades 8-10, age 13-16)

When the students enter lower secondary school, at age 12 or 13, they begin getting grades for their work. Their grades together with their location in the country will determine whether they get accepted at their high school of choice or not. From the eighth grade, the students can choose one elective. Typical subjects the students are offered are the languages German, French and Spanish as well as additional English and Norwegian studies. Before the educational reform starting August 2006, students could choose a practical elective instead of the languages.

Upper Secondary School (*Videregående skole*, age 16-19)

Upper secondary school is 3 years of optional schooling, although recent changes to society and law has made it largely unavoidable in practice.

Secondary education in Norway is primarily based on public

schools: In 2007, 93 per cent of upper secondary school students attended public schools. Until 2005, Norwegian law held private secondary schools to be illegal unless they offered a 'religious or pedagogic alternative', so the only private schools in existence were religious.

Since the introduction of the reform, *the knowledge promotion*, a student will apply for a general studies or a vocational studies path. Inside these main paths there are many sub-paths to follow. The new reform makes the incorporation of IT into the schooling mandatory, many counties (responsible for the public high schools) offer laptops to general studies students for free or for a small fee. Most of them choose to celebrate with lots of parties and festivities, which, impractically, take place a few weeks before the final examinations of the final year.

SWEDEN

Education in Sweden is mandatory for all children from year 7 to the year of the child's 16th birthday. From the age of one, children can be admitted to pre-school *forskola*. Pre-school help to provide an environment that stimulates children's development and learning, and enables parents to combine parenthood with work or studies. During the year before children start compulsory school, all children are offered a place in a pre-school class, which combines the pedagogical methods of the pre-school with those of compulsory school. Between ages 6-7 and 15-16, children attend compulsory comprehensive school (grundskola), divided in three stages.

The vast majority of schools in Sweden are municipally run, but there are also autonomous and publicly funded schools, known as "free schools". The education in free schools has many objectives in common with the municipal school, but it can have an orientation that differs from that of the municipal schools. A handful of boarding schools, known as "private schools", are funded by privately paid tuition.

The Swedish School Plan also highly encourages an individualistic education in which each student has their specific needs met. The students are also encouraged not only to participate in student councils, but also to actually form the education they desire together with their teachers, choosing what books to read and how to balance practice with theory depending on which the individual students find most enjoyable to learn from.

From the autumn of 2011, a new grading system has been introduced into the Swedish school system: A, B, C, D, and E as passing grades and F as Failing. B and D work as filling grades, for when a student hasn't reached all objectives for C or A, but has reached most of them. If the student can't be graded, e.g. extensive truancy, the student will receive a dash instead of F. If a student is given F, they will receive a written review of how to improve themselves.

The quality of Swedish education has been keenly debated over the past decade. As a result, Sweden has implemented school reforms in recent years to improve results and raise the status of the teaching profession.

New Education Act

The Swedish Education Act from 2011 contains basic principles and provisions for compulsory and further education, preschool, kindergarten, out-of school care and adult education. It promotes greater knowledge, freedom of choice, and student safety and security.

New consolidated curricula for compulsory schools for all students, Sami schools, special schools and high schools came into force July 1, 2011. The curricula contain new general goals, guidelines and syllabuses. The preschool curriculum includes clearer goals for children's linguistic and communicative development and for science and technology. Mandatory national subject tests are held in years 3, 6 and 9 of compulsory school to assess student progress. There are also new qualification requirements for areas including high-school studies.

The old Swedish system of Pass (G), Pass with Distinction (VG), Pass with Special Distinction (MVG) and Did Not Pass (IG) has been replaced by a new grading scale with six grades from A to F. A to E are passing grades, with F as a failing grade. Beginning with the fall term of 2012, grades will be assigned starting in year 6.

Introduction of Teacher Certification

Beginning December 1, 2013, professional certification will be required for school and preschool/kindergarten teachers on permanent contracts. The decision, a milestone in Swedish education policy, aims to raise the status of the teaching profession, supporting professional development and thus increasing quality in education.

Ten Years of Schooling

The Swedish Education Act states that all children and young people are to have equal access to education, regardless of gender, where they live or social or economic factors. Attendance at school is compulsory for all children through year 9. Today almost all children also attend non-compulsory kindergarten at the age of six. In practice, this means ten years of education in all.

Pre-school

Pre-school (*förskola*) is open to children from one to five years of age. Municipalities have an obligation to provide such facilities for children whose parents work or study. There have never been as many children in preschool as now. More than eight out of ten children from one to five years of age spend part of their weekdays there. The Swedish tradition of preschool emphasizes the importance of play in a child's development and learning. The interests and needs of children are key components of their education in the preschool curriculum. Gender-aware education is increasingly common in Swedish preschools. The aim is for children to have the same opportunities in life, regardless of gender.

Kindergarten

All children are offered a place in kindergarten (*förskoleklass*) starting in the fall term of the year they turn six until they start compulsory schooling. Kindergarten is designed to stimulate each child's development and learning, and provide a platform for their future schooling.

Elementary School

Elementary school for years 1–3 is followed by middle school for years 4–6 and then junior high school for years 7–9. Children between six and thirteen are also offered out-of-school care before and after school hours. This can be at an after-school center, a family daycare home or an open after-school programme.

Senior High School

Senior high school (*gymnasium*) is optional and free of charge. Senior high school programmes run for three years. Almost all students who finish compulsory school start senior high school. To be accepted into a national programme, students must have passing grades in Swedish or Swedish as a second language, English and mathematics. For senior high school, students require passing grades in nine additional subjects, for a total of twelve. For a vocational programme, students must have passing grades in five additional subjects, for a total of eight.

Free School

Prior to the 1990s, there were only a handful of private schools in Sweden, mostly tuition-funded boarding schools whereof Sigtunaskolan and Lundsbergs skola are the most well known. A major education reform in 1992 allowed privately-run schools offering primary or secondary education to receive public funding for each student, at a level similar to what public schools receive. These are called 'free schools'.

The 'free schools' are funded with public money from the local municipality, based on the number of pupils they have enrolled, in the same way Swedish public schools are. Consequently, they are not allowed to discriminate or require admission examinations, nor are they not allowed to charge the students any additional fees.

Children's Right to Health

All students have access to a school doctor, school nurse, psychologist and school welfare officer at no cost.

Two laws, the Swedish Education Act and the Swedish Discrimination Act, help protect children and students from discrimination and degrading treatment. In essence, the principals of preschools, schools and adult education programmes are responsible for enforcing prohibitions against discrimination and degrading behavior, and for promoting equal treatment. In 2006, Sweden appointed its first Child and School Student Representative, who is tasked with providing information about the discrimination act, helping schools prevent bullying, overseeing schools' efforts and representing students who have been bullied. This position was long the only one of its type in the world, but it is hoped that similar positions will be introduced in other countries as a result of international visits to the representative's office to learn about its work.

Independent Schools

The number of independent schools in Sweden is growing, and today school choice is seen as a right.

The Swedish government supports the establishment of independent schools, which must be approved by the Schools Inspectorate and follow the national curricula and syllabuses. In 2010 roughly 10 per cent of school operations were carried out by private players. Twelve per cent of compulsory school students and 24 per cent of senior high school students attend independent schools. There are also a few international schools whose curricula follow those of other countries. These schools are partly funded by the Swedish government and are mainly aimed at the children of foreign nationals who are in Sweden for a limited time.

The independent school system in Sweden—in which education is free and students have general access to schools with the freedom to choose among a variety of providers—has attracted interest from around the world. In Sweden, some people think it is wrong to run schools for profit, and highlight examples of poor conditions and inconsistencies as a consequence of the system. Advocates of independent schools note the many positive results found in statistical surveys. One is that parents with children who attend independent schools are more satisfied than those with children in municipal schools.

SWITZERLAND

The education system in Switzerland is very diverse, because the Constitution delegates the authority for the school system mainly to the cantons The Swiss constitution sets the foundations, namely that primary school is obligatory for every child and is free in public schools and that the confederation can run or support universities.

The minimum age for primary school is about six years in all cantons but Obwalden, where it is five years and three months. After primary schools, the pupils split up according to their abilities and intentions of career paths. The other students split in two or more school-types (depends on the canton) differing in the balance of theoretical and practical education. It is obligatory for all children to attend school for at least 9 years.

Primary Education

The obligatory school system usually includes primary education. Before that, children usually go to kindergarten, but it is not required. The minimum age for primary school is about six years in all cantons but Obwalden where it is five years and three months. Primary school continues until grade four, five or six, depending on the school. Any boy or girl can take part in school if they choose to, but pupils are separated depending on whether they speak French, German or Italian.

Secondary School

At the end of primary school, pupils are separated according to their capacities and career-intentions in several (often three) sections. Students who aspire to an academic career enter high schools to be prepared for further studies. Students intending to pursue a trade or vocation complete only three additional years before entering vocational education which are regulated by federal law and are based on a cooperation of private business offering educational job-positions and public schools offering obligatory school-lessons complimentary to the on the job-education. This so-called "dual system" splitting academic and vocational training has its continuation in the higher education system

In the lower secondary level there are several different teaching and school models that may exist. Some cantons define a specific model, while others allow the individual municipalities to determine which model to follow.

Separated Model

Pupils are allocated to institutionally separate school types, according to their performance levels. The structure is based on the principle of equal capacities among pupils. Generally, each school type has its own adapted curricula, teaching material, teachers and, in some cases, its own range of subjects.

The cooperative model is based on core classes with different performance requirements. Each pupil is assigned to a core class according to his or her performance level. The pupils attend lessons in certain subjects in differentiated requirement-based groups (whereby the core classes are mixed).

The integrated model does not use different school types or core classes. Pupils with different performance levels attend the same class and mixing is maintained. In certain subjects, teaching occurs on differentiated requirement-based levels.

UNITED KINGDOM

Education in the United Kingdom is a devolved matter with each of the countries of the United Kingdom having separate systems under separate governments: the UK government is responsible for England, and the Scottish government, the Welsh government and the Northern Ireland Executive are responsible for Scotland, Wales and Northern Ireland respectively.

Primary education is provided by state schools run by the government and by independent fee-paying schools. In the state system children are either educated in separate infant and junior schools or in a combined primary school. Schools in the private sector providing primary education are generally known as preparatory schools or prep schools. In the private sector the transfer to the final stage of education.

There have been great changes in the educational system in Great Britain since 1988. A few education acts have been issued (from 1988 to 1994) to raise standards at all ability levels, to give parents a wider choice of schools and to make further and higher education more economically available to large numbers of people.

All children and young people between the age of 5 and 16 must get full-time education. Over 90 per cent of all school children attend schools maintained from public funds (state schools).

Although overall responsibility rests with central government, most of these schools are financed and maintained by Local Education Authorities (LEAs). Education at these schools is free. Every publicly maintained school has a governing body which includes members appointed by LEAs, teachers and parents. Besides this state system of education there are also fee-paying independent schools -private and church (for about seven per cent of children). Both types of schools are subject to official inspection. Boys and girls are taught together at most primary schools and more than 80 per cent of pupils at state secondary schools attend mixed schools (in Northern Ireland it is less, in Scotland almost all secondary schools are coeducational). Most independent schools for younger pupils are mixed but the majority of private secondary schools are single-sex.

The state system of education is divided into four stages: pre-school and primary education, secondary education, further education and higher education.

Pre-school Education

Pre-school education is provided by nursery schools. In England over one half of three- and four-year olds attend school and many other children attend pre-school playgroups, mostly organized by parents. (In Wales more than 70 per cent do so, while in Northern Ireland only about 15 per cent, but about 45 per cent start their compulsory schooling at 4). There are not enough state nursery schools in Britain and people have campaigned for a long time to get more opened. There are private nurseries but these are expensive and a lot of families cannot afford them. Children start at 9 a.m. and finish at 3 p.m., they have their lunch at school and usually a rest in the afternoon. They play, paint, dance and sing and do the same things that all little children do. They do not have proper lessons.

Primary Education

Primary education is provided by primary schools. The infant school has its own building and playground and is next to the junior school, with its own building and playground. So, although you move up into junior school at 7 you do not have to change completely. There are usually about 35 children in a class and, in the infant school, as well as a teacher, there is usually a teacher's assistant. Also mothers (and occasionally, fathers) often go into the Infant Schools to help with painting, reading and practical lessons. Emphasis in the infant school is on learning through experience, through drawing, painting, musical activities, movement and play. Children learn to read, write a little and do simple counting.

Classrooms are bright and cheerful with children's work displayed on the walls and books, games and a computer in each classroom. The children usually sit in groups at tables and have drawers to keep their work in. At 7 many children move to junior school or departments, where the work is more systematic. Children learn English, mathematics, science and technology, geography and religious knowledge. A lot of learning is done through project or topic work, with an emphasis on children finding things out for themselves. They also learn about the environment and, of course, do art, music and Physicaleducation. Children have the same teacher for one year and she teaches nearly all of the lessons in the class. Perhaps another teacher has them once a week for music or physical training. The government is discussing changing this so that there are more specialist teachers in the Junior Schools. The children would then have different teachers for different lessons. The usual age for transfer from primary school to secondary school is 11 (12 in Scotland).

Secondary Education

At the age of 11 pupils transfer from primary school to secondary school. About 90 per cent of state secondary school pupils go to Comprehensive schools. These were introduced in 1960s and the word "comprehensive" means all-inclusive. Most of these schools are very large and vary in size, 900 to 1,500 pupils is the most common. They take children of all abilities and provide a wide range of secondary education, both academic and practical, for all or most of the children in a district within the 11-to 18- age range (12 to 18 in Scotland).

About four per cent of children attend Grammar Schools which they enter at the age of 11 on the basis of their abilities. Grammar Schools offer a mainly academic education for the 11 to 18 or 19-year age group. Six per cent of children attend Secondary Modern Schools which provide a more general education up to the age of 16, although pupils can stay beyond the minimum leaving age. Education in England is overseen by the Department of Education and the Department of Business, Innovation and Skills. Local authorities (LAs) take responsibility for implementing policy for public education and state schools at a regional level. The education system is divided into nursery (ages 3–4), primary education (ages 4–11), secondary education (ages 11–18) and tertiary education (ages 18+).

Full-time education is compulsory for all children aged between 5 and 16, with a child beginning primary education during the school year he or she turns 5. Students may then continue their secondary studies for a further two years (sixth form), leading most typically to A-level qualifications, although other qualifications and courses exist.

Education by Means other than Schooling

The Education Act requires parents to ensure their children are educated either by attending school or alternative means. Small but increasing numbers of parents are choosing to educate their children by means other than schooling. This style of education is often referred to as Elective Home Education. The education can take a variety of forms ranging from homeschooling where a school-style curriculum is followed at home, to unschooling, where any semblance of structure in the educational provision is abandoned. Parents do not need permission to educate their own children. There is no requirement for parents to follow the National Curriculum, or to give formal lessons. Parents do not need to be qualified teachers, or to follow school hours and terms. Parents who choose to educate their children outside of school must finance their children's education themselves.

Further Education

Students at both state schools and independent schools typically take GCSE examinations, which mark the end of compulsory education. Above school-leaving age, the independent and state sectors are similarly structured. In the 16–18 age group, sixth form education is not compulsory at present.

NORTHERN IRELAND

Education in Northern Ireland differs from systems used elsewhere in the United Kingdom though it is more similar to that used in Wales than it is to Scotland. A child's age on 1 July determines the point of entry into the relevant stage of education unlike England and Wales where it is the 1 September. Northern Ireland's results at GCSE and A-Level are consistently top in the UK. At A-Level, one third of students in Northern Ireland achieved A grades in 2007, which is a higher proportion than in England and Wales. The Northern Ireland Executive Department is responsible for the country's education policy except for the higher and further education sector. The Department of Education's main areas of responsibility cover pre-school, primary, post-primary and special education; the youth service; the promotion of community relations within and between schools; and teacher education and salaries. Its primary statutory duty is to promote the education of the people of Northern Ireland and to ensure the effective implementation of education policy.

Curriculum

All schools in Northern Ireland follow the Northern Ireland Curriculum which is based on the National Curriculum used in England and Wales. At age 11, on entering secondary education, all pupils study a broad base of subjects which include geography, English, mathematics, science, physical education, music and modern languages. Currently there are proposals to reform the curriculum to make its emphasis more skills-based under which, in addition to those mentioned, home economics, local and global citizenship and personal, social and health education would become compulsory subjects. At age 14, pupils select which subjects to continue to study for General Certificate of Secondary Education (GCSE) examinations. Currently it is compulsory to study English, mathematics and religious studies, although a full

GCSE course does not have to be studied for the latter. In addition, pupils usually elect to continue with other subjects and many study for eight or nine GCSEs but possibly up to ten or eleven. GCSEs mark the end of compulsory education in Northern Ireland.

Controlled schools (nursery, primary, special, secondary modern and grammar schools) are under the management of the school's board of governors and the employing authorities are the five education and library boards. Although open to those of all faiths and none, many of these schools were originally church schools, whose control was transferred to the state in the first half of the twentieth century.

SCOTLAND

Traditionally, the Scottish system at *secondary school* level has emphasized breadth across a range of subjects, while the *English, Welsh* and *Northern Irish* systems have emphasized greater depth of education over a smaller range of subjects.

Scotland has a long history of universal provision of public education, and the Scottish education system is distinctly different from the other countries of the United Kingdom. The Scotland Act 1998 gives Scottish Parliament legislative control over all education matters, and Education Act the principal legislation governing education in Scotland.

Children start primary school aged between 4½ and 5½ depending on when the child's birthday falls. Scottish school policy places all those born between March of a given year and February of the following year in the same year group. Children born between March and August start school in August at between 5½ and 5 years old, and those born between September and February start school in the previous August at between age 4 years 11 months and 4½ years old.

The Scottish system is the most flexible in the UK, however, as parents of children born between September and December can request a deferral for 1 year (not automatic, requires to be approved), whilst children born between January and February can opt to hold their child back a year and let them start school the following August. This usually allows those not ready for formal education to have an extra year at nursery school.

Pupils remain at primary school for seven years. Then aged

eleven or twelve, they start secondary school for a compulsory four years with the following two years being optional. It is now required by the Scottish Parliament for students to have two hours of physical education a week; each school may vary the compulsory combinations.

Access to Nursery, Primary and Secondary School

Government funded schools are free for children aged 5-16. In many cases, this applies to children of international post-graduate students, and other immigrants. The age ranges specify the youngest age for a child entering that year and the oldest age for a child leaving that year. Children may start attending nursery as soon as they have passed their third birthday, and progress to Primary 1 in the August of the year in which they turn five. In general, the cut-off point for ages is the end of February, so all children must be of a certain age on 1 March in order to begin class in August. Children may leave school once they reach their statutory school leaving date; this is dependent on date of birth.

Which high school the child goes to depends on the area they live in, known as the "Catchment Area" which has a specific high school which takes children. Parents can also apply for a placing request if they would like their child to go to a school outside their Catchment area, and a panel will decide if the child is the most worthy child.

WALES

Education in Wales is compulsory between the ages of 5 to 16 and they have about 1900 state schools offering free education to more than 470,000 pupils. Another 65,000 students between 16 and 19 are in vocational training in further education institutions. A number of overseas pupils are also enrolled in our private fee-paying schools

A significant number of students all over Wales are educated either wholly or largely through the medium of Welsh and lessons in the language are compulsory for all until the age of 16. Welsh medium education is available to all age groups from nursery through to schools, colleges, universities and adult education.

Education in Wales differs in certain respects from education elsewhere in the UK. For example, a small number of students all over Wales are educated either wholly or largely through the medium of Welsh. Welsh medium of education is available to all age groups through nurseries, schools, colleges and universities and in adult education; lessons in the language itself are compulsory for all pupils until the age of 16.

A child's age on the 1 September determines the point of entry into the relevant stage of education. Education is compulsory beginning with the term following the child's fifth (third in Wales) birthday, but may take place at either home or school. Most parents choosing to educate through school-based provision, however, enroll their children in the reception year in September of that school year, with most children thus beginning school at age four or four and a half.

Primary Education

In 2008 a unique new curriculum—the Foundation phase—was rolled out to all schools in Wales. It began for 3- to 4-year-olds and by 2011 is in place for 3- to 7-year-olds. It is based on experiential learning, in small groups, with a teacher ratio of 1:8 for the youngest ages. It has been acclaimed as 'one of the most significant acts of the Welsh government since it was formed' and has been almost universally welcomed.

They will be given time to develop their speaking and listening skills and to become confident in their reading and writing abilities. Mathematics will be more practical so that children can see how problems are solved and how important mathematics is in their everyday lives. There will be more emphasis on children understanding how things work and on finding different ways to solve problems. The curriculum will focus on experiential learning, active involvement and developing each child's Skills and understanding, Personal, social, emotional, physical and intellectual well being so as to develop the whole child;

REFERENCES

Education Act (1985:1100)" (PDF). Swedish Government Offices. 1985-12-12.

Education in Flanders: A broad view of the Flemish educational landscape, Ministry of the Flemish community, 2005

http://archiv.sueddeutsche.de/957389/882/2789903/Studium-mit-dem-Meisterbrief.html

http://www.bbc.co.uk/news/uk-wales-11930257

http://www.buckingham.ac.uk/research/ceer/publications

http://www.lobo.nl/openbaaronderwijsenbijzonderonderwijs/

http://www.muellerscience.com/SPEZIALITAETEN/Schweiz/SchweizerNobelpreistraeger.htm

http://www.ond.vlaanderen.be/hogeronderwijs/werken/studentadmin/mededeling-gegevensbeheer/md20090325studiegeld0910.htm

http://www.scis.org.uk/assets/files/2011%20Local%20Authority%20comparisons%20by%t20region

http:/2.www.ireland.anglican.org/cmsfiles/pdf/Information/Submissions/TRC/trc_aec_2711

Learning for Tomorrows World—First Results from PISA 2003, OECD, 2004

Niikko, A. (2006) "Finnish Daycare: Caring, Education and Instruction", in *Nordic Childhoods and Early Education: Philosophy, Research, Policy and Practice in Denmark, Finland, Iceland, Norway, and Sweden, Series: International Perspectives on Educational Policy, Research*

www.citizensinformation.ie

www.skl.se – Swedish Association of Local Authorities and Regions (SALAR)

www.skolinspektionen.se – Swedish Schools Inspectorate (Statens skolinspektion)

www.skolmatensvanner.se – Friends of Swedish School Meals

www.skolverket.se – National Agency for Education (Skolverket)

5

Elementary Education in Africa

According to UNESCO's *Regional overview on sub-Saharan Africa,* in 2000, 52 per cent of children were enrolled in primary schools, the lowest enrollment rate of any region. UNESCO also reported marked gender inequalities: In most parts of Africa there is much higher enrollment by boys; in some there are more girls, due to sons having to stay home and tend to the family farm. Africa has more than 40 million children, almost half the school-age child population, receiving no schooling. Two-thirds of these are girls. The USAID Center reports that as of 2005, 40 per cent of school-age children in Africa do not attend primary school and there are still 46 million school-age African children who have never stepped into a classroom.

The regional report produced by the UNESCO-BREDA education sector analyst team in 2005 indicates that less than 10 per cent of African children are now allowed in the system. Four out of 10 children did not complete primary school in 2002-2003. So, five years after the World Education Forum and the adoption of the Millennium Goals, progress at primary level is far from decisive. The analysis highlights that principal efforts should be directed to reducing the number of dropouts per level. It appears also that geographical disparities (rural areas/urban areas) or economic disparities (low income households/wealthy households) are more significant and take longer to even out than gender disparities. From the quality point of view, studies such as SACMEQ (Southern and Eastern Africa Consortium for Monitoring Educational Quality) and household surveys indicate very significant disparities in performance between and within countries

Education in Africa began as a tool to prepare the local youth to take their place in their respective societies and not necessarily for life outside of Africa. In some areas, the pre-European colonialism schooling system consisted of groups of older people teaching aspects and rituals that would help them in adulthood. In other areas, education in early African societies included such things as artistic performances, ceremonies, games, festivals, dancing, singing and drawing. Boys and girls were taught separately to help prepare each sex for their adult roles. Every member of the community had a hand in contributing to the educational upbringing of the child. The high point of the education experience in certain societies in Africa was the ritual passage ceremony from childhood to adulthood.

When European colonialism and imperialism took place it began to change many indigenous education systems. Schooling was no longer just about rituals and rites of passage, school would now mean earning an education that would allow Africans to compete with countries such as the United States and those in Europe. Africa would begin to try producing their own educated students as other countries had.

Education participation rates in many African countries are low. Schools often lack many basic facilities, and African universities suffer from overcrowding and staff being lured away to Western countries by higher pay and better conditions.

It was also showed that secondary (lower and higher levels) and higher education enrollments have progressed proportionally more than primary enrollment over the period 1990–2003 which questions the reality of policy priority given to primary education. The strong pressure for education continuity from the majority already benefiting from schooling explains this trend. To this must be added the weakness of mechanisms regulating pupil flow between the different levels of the education system.

In 2005, the inventory and trends show a definitive risk of not reaching universal primary enrollment by 2015. 14.7 per cent of the world's population is in Africa.

The education systems inherited from the colonial powers were designed for the formal sector and public administration. However, ADEA (Association for the Development of Education in Africa) has become aware of the informal sector's relevance in developing countries, and thus recognized the need for increased vocational school training as a way to help the informal sector.

Lack of Proper Schooling Facilities and Educators

The main reason for the low education rates in Africa is the lack of proper schooling facilities and unequal opportunity for education across countries. Many schools across Africa find it hard to employ teachers due to the low pay and lack of suitable people. This is particularly true for schools in remote areas. Most people who manage to receive education would prefer to move to big cities or even overseas where more opportunities and higher pay await. Thus, there will be an overly large class sizes and high average number of students per teacher in a school. Moreover, the teachers are usually those unqualified with few teaching aids and poor textbook provision. Due to this, children attending schools in rural areas usually attain poorer results in standardized tests compared to their urban counterparts. This can be seen in the reports given by the Southern and Eastern Africa Consortium for Monitoring Educational Quality (SACMEQ). Those taking the tests in rural areas score much lower than those in small towns and big cities. This shows a lack of equal education opportunity given to children from different parts of the same country.

Emigration

Next, emigration leads to a loss of highly educated people and financial loss. The loss of skilled people can only be replaced with another huge cost which imply the loss of money spent educating people who leave and new people to replace them. Even though an almost 5.5 per cent of GDP investment in education, the loss makes it difficult for the government to budget another amount in education as they will need to prioritize other needs such as military budget and debt servicing.

Military and Conflict

Military spending is causing education spending to decrease immensely. According to a March 2011 report by UNESCO, armed conflicts the biggest threat to education in Africa. While the number of dropouts across the continent has been increasing dramatically, one of the influences of war and conflict on education is the diversion of public funds from education to military spending. An already underfunded system is losing more money. Twenty-one African countries have been identified as the highest spenders of gross domestic product on military globally compared with the amount directed toward education. Military and conflict also leads to the displacement of children. It often forces them to remain in camps or flee to their neighboring countries where education is not available to them.

In Kenya, after disputed national elections in December 2007, civil unrest displaced over 250,000 people and affected a total of 500,000 persons. The Ministry of Education statistics indicate 62,848 of primary school going children were affected by the ensuing violence.

Corruption in Education

A 2010 Transparency International Report with research gathered from 8,500 educators and parents in Ghana, Madagascar, Morocco, Niger, Senegal, Sierra leone, and Uganda, found that education is being denied to African children in incredibly large numbers

A lack of parent involvement, especially as an overseer of government activities also leads to enormous corruption. This was most often found to be because parents and communities feel as though they lack any kind of power in regard to their child's education. In Uganda only 50 per cent of parents believe that they have the power to influence decisions regarding the education of their child. In Morocco, just 20 per cent of parents believed they held any sort of power.

The unavailability and incompleteness of records in schools and districts prevents the documentation and prevention of corrupt practices. The African Education Watch conducted surveys all over the continent and identified the three most common practices of corruption:

Illegal Collection of Fees: One part of their research focused on of so-called registration fees. Parents from every country surveyed reported paying even though, by law, primary schooling is free. The report found that the number of parents forced to pay these illegal accounting fees

Embezzlement of school funds: In the study, Transparency International found that 64 per cent of the schools surveyed on the continent published no financial information at all.

Power abuse: Another major problem is incompetent

management. The report found that in many schools the little resources they did have being wasted or lost. Overall, 85 per cent of schools across all countries had either deficient accounting systems or none at all. In Morocco, just 23 per cent of head teachers received training in financial management, despite being responsible for budgets. The TI report found that there was sexual abuse in schools from teachers. The TI report also found that many schools were plagued by teacher absenteeism and alcoholism.

Without this basic education, the report found it was nearly impossible to go on to high school or college. African children are missing this link that allows them to have a chance in trade or to go beyond their villages.

NGOs' Involvement

A report by USAID and the Bureau for Africa, Office of Sustainable Development, found that NGOs are increasingly participating in contribute to the delivery of education services, education policy decisions and are included by donors and government officials in many parts of the education system. Of course, this varies country to country and region to region.

NGOs working in education in Africa often encountered tension and competition when working. Schools, parents and, most often government officials, feel threatened by third-party involvement and feel that they are "crashing the party." The report continues that for NGOs to be effective, they must understand that they do not have the same perspective as government officials as to who is in control. If they do not recognize the government of the country they are working in, they will compromise their objectives.

To be effective in education in Africa NGOs must effect policy and create policy changes that support their projects. NGOs also found that, to see this policy change that they are striving for, they must create and foster relationships with many different stakeholders. The most important stakeholders are usually donors and government officials. The biggest challenge for NGOs has been linking these networks together. NGO interventions to change policy have revealed that NGO programmes have failed to create a successful way to change the policy process while making sure that the public understands and is a part of education policy. This problem will prove more influential in the future if it is not solved.

Women's Education

A positive correlation exists between the enrollment of girls in primary school and the gross national product and increase of life expectancy.

In 2000, 93.4 million women in Sub Saharan Africa were illiterate. Many reasons exist for why formal education for females is unavailable to so many, including cultural reasons. For example, some believe that a women's education will get in the way of her duties as a wife and a mother. In some places in Africa where women marry at age 12 or 13, education is considered a hindrance to a young woman's development.

Women's education is sometimes corrupted by sexual violence. Sexual violence against girls and female students affects many African education systems. In Sub-Saharan Africa, sexual violence is one of the most common and least known forms of corruption.

Disparity in Education

While most of the Millennium Development Goals face a deadline of 2015, the gender parity target was set to be achieved a full ten years earlier—an acknowledgement that equal access to education is the foundation for all other development goals. Gender disparity is defined as inequalities of some quantity attributed to the reason of gender type. In countries where resources and school facilities are lacking, and total enrollments are low, a choice must often be made in families between sending a girl or a boy to school. Of an estimated 101 million children not in school, more than half are girls. However, this statistic increased when examining secondary school education. In high-income countries, 95 per cent as many girls as boys attend primary and secondary schools. However, in sub-Saharan Africa the figure is just 60 per cent.

The foremost factor limiting female education is poverty. Economic poverty plays a key role when it comes to coping with direct costs such as tuition fees, cost of textbooks, uniforms, transportation and other expenses. Wherever, especially in families with many children, these costs exceed the income of the family, girls are the first to be denied schooling. This gender bias decision in sending females to school is also based on gender roles dictated by culture. Girls usually are required to complete household chores or take care of their younger siblings when they reach home. This limits there time to study and in many cases, may even have to miss school to complete their duties. It is common for girls to be taken out of school at this point. Boys however, may be given more time to study if their parents believe that the education will allow them to earn more in the future. Expectations, attitudes and biases in communities and families, economic costs, social traditions, and religious and cultural beliefs limit girls' educational opportunities.

Whatever the underlying reason(s) are, about having large numbers of girls outside the formal schooling system brings developmental challenges to both current and future generations. According to the UNESCO, the rates of female children out of primary school is higher than that of male children in all the African countries where data is available. Until equal numbers of girls and boys are in school, it will be impossible to build the knowledge necessary to eradicate poverty and hunger, combat disease and ensure environmental sustainability. Millions of children and women will continue to die needlessly, placing the rest of the development agenda at risk.

Selected country wide description of Education in Africa is presented below:

EGYPT

In Egypt, there is special attention given by the government and other NGOs to reduce gender disparity in education and to achieve the 2015 MDG of universal primary education.

The Egyptian educational system is highly centralized, and is divided into three stages:

- Basic Education,
- Primary Stage,
- Preparatory Stage

Since Egypt's extension of the free compulsory education law in 1981 to include the Preparatory Stage, both Primary and Preparatory phases (Ages 6 through 14) have been combined together under the label Basic Education. Education beyond this stage depends on the student's ability.

Egypt has the largest overall education system in the North

Antartica (MENA) and it has grown rapidly since the early 1990s. In recent years the Government of Egypt has accorded even greater priority in improving the education system. According to the Human Development Index (HDI), Egypt is ranked 123 in the HDI, and 7 in the lowest 10 HDI countries in the Middle East and Northern Africa, in 2009. With the help of World Bank and other multilateral organizations Egypt aims to increase access in early childhood care and education and the inclusion of ICT at all levels of education, especially at the tertiary level.

The Ministry of education is also tackling with a number of issues: trying to move from a highly centralized system to offering more autonomy to individual institutions, thereby increasing accountability. The personnel management in the education also needs to be overhauled and teachers should be hired on merit with salaries attached to the performance.

Education System

The public education system in Egypt consists of three levels:

- Basic education stage for 4–14 years old
- Kindergarten for two years followed by
- Primary school for six years and
- Preparatory school for three years.

Then, the secondary school stage is for three years, for ages 15 to 17, followed by the tertiary level. Education is made compulsory for 9 academic years between the ages of 6 and 14. Moreover, all levels of education are free for any government run schools.

Egypt launched its National Strategic Plan for Pre-University Education Reform (2007/08-2011/12) The Strategic Plan (which has the subtitle 'Towards an educational paradigm shift') mirrors Egypt's commitment to a comprehensive, sustainable, and collective approach towards ensuring an education of quality for all and developing a knowledge society.

Its key elements are: i) access and participation ii) teachers iii) pedagogy iv) curriculum and learning assessment v) text books and learning materials vi) management and governance and vii) a quality improvement strategy.

Promotional examinations are held at all levels except in grades 3, 6 and 9 at the basic education level and the grades 11 and 12 in the secondary stage, which apply standardized regional or national exams.

Types of Schools

Government Schools

Generally speaking, there are two types of government Schools

- *Arabic Schools*, provide the governmental national curriculum in the Arabic language. A governmental English language curriculum is taught starting at first Primary year and either French, German, Spanish or Italian is added as a second foreign language in Secondary Education.
- *Experimental Language Schools*, teach most of the government curriculum (Science, Mathematics and Computer) in English, and adds French or German as a second foreign language in Preparatory Education. An Advanced English language curriculum is provided in all Educational stages, Except for the last two years. Social Studies are taught in Arabic. Students are admitted into first grade at age seven; a year older than Arabic schools.

Private Schools

Generally speaking, there are four types of private schools.

- *Ordinary Schools*, their curriculum is quite similar to that of the government schools, but the private schools pay more attention to the students' personal needs and to the school facilities.
- *Language Schools*, teach most of the government curriculum in English, and add French or German as a second foreign language. They are expected to be better than the other schools, because of the facilities available, but their fees are much higher. Some of these schools use French or German as their main language of instruction, but it may be difficult for the student to study in governmental universities in Arabic or English afterward.
- *Religious Schools*, are religiously oriented schools as Azhar schools or Catholic schools.

- *International Schools,* are private schools that follow another country's curriculum, like British, American, or French system, and the degrees earned from them get official certification from the Ministry of Education, to be eligible to enroll in Egyptian universities, such schools offer even better facilities & activities than regular private schools with higher fees, but are criticized to be providing a much easier education level compared to the general curriculum, and some Egyptian universities require higher grades than those of regular schools students as a minimum for enrollment, or an extra high school certificate like SAT.

Basic Education

The basic education consists of pre-primary, primary and preparatory levels of education. Irrespective of private or state run, all preschool institutions come under Ministry of Education. It is the Ministry's duty to select and distribute textbooks. According to the Ministry's guidelines, the maximum size of a preschool should not exceed more than 45 students. Ministry of Education is also getting support from the international agencies, such as the World Bank to enhance the early childhood education system by increasing access to schools, improving quality of education and building capacity of teachers.

The second tier of basic compulsory education is the preparatory stage or lower secondary which is three years long. Completion of this tier grants students the Basic Education Completion Certificate.

Secondary Education

Secondary education consists of three tracks: general, vocational/ technical and the dual system vocational education which represented in Mubarak Kohl schools. The general secondary stage includes 3 years of education, whereas the secondary vocational track could be for 3–5 years and 3 years for the dual system vocational education. To enter the secondary level, the students must pass a national exam which is given at end of the secondary stage. At this level, students have formative and summative assessments during the first year and the average of the end of year national standardized exams for year two and three qualifies the students to take the Certificate of General Secondary Education, which is one of the requirements for admission into the universities. Secondary education consists of three different types: general, technical or vocational.

Al-Azhar System

Another system that runs in parallel with the public educational system is known as the Al-Azhar system. It consists of six years of primary stage, a three year preparatory stage and finally three years of secondary stage. The Ministry of education reduced the number of secondary school years from four to three years in 1998, so as to align the Al Azhar system with the general secondary education system. In this system as well, there are separate schools for girls and boys. Al Azhar education system is supervised by the "Supreme Council of the Al-Azhar Institution".

All schools in all stages teach religious subjects and non-religious subjects, to a certain degree- not as intensively as the state schools. The bulk of the curriculum, however, consists of religious subjects as described below. All the students are Muslims, and males and females are separated in the prep and secondary stages. Al-Azhar schools are all over the country, especially in rural areas. The graduates of Al-Azhar secondary schools are eligible to continue their studies at the Al-Azhar University.

ETHIOPIA

Ethiopia faces many historical, cultural, social and political obstacles that have restricted progress in education for many centuries. According to UNESCO reviews, most people in Ethiopia feel that work is more important than education, so they start at a very early age with little to no education. Children in rural areas are less likely to go to school than children in urban areas. Though gradually improving, most rural families cannot afford to send their children to school because parents believe that while their children are in school they cannot contribute to the household chores and income. Social awareness that education is important is something that Ethiopia lacks but has improved gradually. There is a need to change the importance of education in the country's social structure, and children should be encouraged and required to attend school and become educated.

The sequence of general education in Ethiopia is eight years of primary school, two years of lower secondary school and two years of higher secondary school.

The society of Ethiopia expects teachers and parents to use corporal punishment to maintain order and discipline. Most believe that through punishing children for bad habits they in turn learn good ones. Many educated Ethiopians seek higher salaries in foreign countries thus many of those who manage to finish higher education emigrate from Ethiopia creating an endless shortage of qualified professionals in every sector of the country.

Benefiting from sustained growth, the Ethiopian government, in partnership with donors, has invested heavily in improving access to education. Key measures have included abolishing school fees, increasing expenditure on school construction and maintenance and hiring and training thousands of new teachers, administrators and officials. This has been complemented by a shift to mother tongue instruction and by the gradual decentralization of the education system to progressively lower administrative levels. This has likely contributed to improved service delivery.

Ethiopia's progress in education demonstrates that a sustained government-led effort to reduce poverty and expand the public education system equitably, backed by sufficient resources and improved service delivery, can dramatically increase school enrolment.

Sustained Government Commitment

Government priorities in education—increasing enrolment and access in rural areas (with a goal of achieving universal primary enrolment by 2015), gender equality and curriculum reform—have been grounded in efforts to improve economic and human development outcomes. Commitment to improving the education system has been matched by substantial increases in the education budget. Public spending on education, which during the 1980s remained under 10 per cent of total spending, had increased to 23.6 per cent of total expenditure by 2008-09. This constitutes 5.5 per cent of gross domestic product (GDP), one of the highest rates on the continent.

The government's prioritisation of education has translated into a number of policies aimed at increasing access to schooling for all Ethiopians, and particularly marginalised groups such as girls, the rural poor and pastoral communities

Increased Community Participation

Increased community involvement has further improved the education system. Many Ethiopians have shown an increased willingness to dedicate scarce resources—including through financial contributions and time—to further improving local schools. These had spent the previous two years on advocacy, school construction and encouraging parents to send their children to schools, although concerns have been raised about the frequently coercive pressure they applied.

KENYA

After independence in 1963, Kenya began a campaign for free primary education Since then, the system of education has undergone transformation twice. Before independence elementary education was based on the colonial system of education. In 1967, Kenya, with Uganda and Tanzania formed the East African Community. The three countries adopted a single system of education.

Education quality has recently received a lot of attention in Kenya. The government's main document in this effort, the Kenya Education Sector Support Programme for 2005–2010, established the National Assessment Centre (NAC) to monitor learning achievement. In 2010, the NAC released the results of its first assessment.

In 2009, in collaboration with the NAC, Uwezo Kenya conducted an assessment of the basic literacy and numeracy skills of children ages 6–16. The ALA was set at a Standard 2 level, which is the level where students are supposed to achieve basic competency in reading English and Kiswahili and complete simple arithmetic problems.

Key findings about education in Kenya, based on the results of the Uwezo 2009 assessment are the following:

- Literacy levels are low, and are substantially lower in certain regions. Girls tend to perform better in reading English and Kiswahili, while boys tend to perform better in math.

- Literacy levels are lower in public schools than private schools.
- Most children can solve real world, "ethno-mathematics" problems, while fewer can solve similar math problems in an abstract, pencil and paper format.
- 5 per cent of children are not enrolled in school, but the problem is far worse in particular regions.
- About half of children are enrolled in pre-school.
- Many children are older than expected for their class level, including 40 per cent of children in class 2, and 60 per cent of children in class 7.
- North Eastern Province and arid districts in Rift Valley and Eastern Provinces have particularly low performance; and many older children, especially girls, are not attending school.
- Many families pay for extra tuition, which focuses heavily on drilling and exam preparation.
- Schools struggle to plan their budgets because they receive funds at unpredictable times.
- Children whose mothers are educated, particularly beyond primary school, tend to have much higher rates of literacy and numeracy.
- About 15 per cent of students are absent on a given day, with much higher absenteeism in certain districts.
- There is a severe shortage of teachers, estimated at 4 teachers per school.

Primary Education

Primary education in Kenya begins at the age of 6 or 7 after completion of a year of kindergarten commonly known as Nursery School or pre-unit. The first class or year of primary school is known as Standard 1, the final year as Standard 8 and primary school children are known as pupils. At the end of the school year students advance to the next grade. Students who completely fail their end of year exams usually repeat the class the following year instead of advancing to a higher grade. Most primary schools are day schools with pupils living at home. Fewer schools at primary level are boarding schools compared to secondary schools. All public primary school pupils sit for the Kenya Certificate of Primary Education examination at the end of the school year in Standard eight.

Secondary Education

Secondary schools in Kenya fall into three categories—government funded, 'harambee' and private. Government funded schools are divided into national, provincial and district levels. Harambee schools do not receive full funding from the government and private schools are run by private organizations or individuals. After taking the primary school leaving exam and successfully passing, government funded schools select students in order of scores. Students with the highest scores gain admission into national schools while those with average scores are selected into provincial and district schools. A number of students also drop out of school by choice due to poor scores.

Under the current system, students attend secondary school for four years before sitting for the school leaving exam at the end of the fourth year. In 2008, the government introduced plans to offer free Secondary education to all Kenyans.

Factors Affecting Education in Kenya

In 1963 the Kenyan government promised free primary education to its citizens. In the early 70s primary school fees were abolished but in the mid 80s cost-sharing measures between the government and its citizens led to the re-introduction of minor fee charges by primary schools. As the trend continued with schools requiring parents to pay fees such as PTA, textbooks, uniforms, caution fees, exam fees and extracurricular activity fees, most parents became overburdened and unable to raise such fees. Those who could not afford the money to pay for their children's school fees often had their children drop out of the school. Many children were also forced to drop out of school when teachers would not allow them to take exams. To pressurize parents to pay fees, schools often sent children home during the final exams.

The growth of Kenya's education sector has exceeded expectations. After the first university was established in 1970, six other public universities and 23 private universities have been established. Although Kenya has its own universities, some parents prefer to send their children to universities outside the country. This is largely because Kenyan public universities are not as flexible with admission requirements as some foreign universities.

NIGERIA

Nigeria has made considerable progress in the domain of education. The education system in the country is supervised by the state. There are 27 federal and state-owned polytechnics in Nigeria. The first 6 years of primary education are mandatory in Nigeria. Nigeria is making a steady progress in the development of education. Many universities and schools have been established by the state. However, much still needs to be done.

Primary education in Nigeria is in the native language but brings in English in the third year. Higher Education has developed considerably over the years, which has resulted in a healthy literacy rate.

Certain important facts about Nigerian Education are:

- Education in Nigeria is managed by the state.
- There are 27 federal and state-owned polytechnics in Nigeria
- The present literacy rate is estimated at 72 per cent.
- The first 6 years of primary education are mandatory in Nigeria

At present, along with a number of state universities, colleges, and schools, the Nigerian local and state governments manage primary and secondary education. Higher education in Nigeria is the responsibility of both the federal and the state governments.

The formal education system in Nigeria includes:

- 6 years of primary schooling
- 3 years of junior secondary schooling
- 3 years of senior secondary schooling, and
- 4 years of university education, finally directing toward a bachelor's level degree in the majority of the subjects.

The annual term of school in Nigeria is ten months, and is sectioned into three ten- to twelve-week periods, each at the pre-primary, primary, junior and senior secondary stages.

The Nigerian education system started slowly but soundly developing during the colonial time until the conclusion of World War II. The Christian missionaries introduced the western education system in Nigeria in the mid-nineteenth century. In 1990, three fundamentally distinct education systems existed in Nigeria—the indigenous system, the Quranic schools, and formal European-style educational institutions.

Education in Nigeria is overseen by the Ministry of Education and the local authorities take responsibility for implementing policy for state controlled public education and state schools at a regional level. The education system is divided into Kindergarten, Primary education, Secondary Education and Tertiary education

Primary Education

Primary education begins at the age of 4 for the majority of Nigerians. Students spend six years in primary school and graduate with a school-leaving certificate. Subjects taught at the primary level include mathematics, English language, Christian Religious Knowledge, Islamic knowledge studies, science and one of the three main indigenous languages and cultures, Hausa-Fulani, Yoruba, and Igbo. Private schools would also offer Computer science, French, and Fine Arts. Primary school students are required to take a Common Entrance Examination to qualify for admission into the Federal and State Government Secondary schools, as well as private ones.

The Universal Basic Education, *UBE*, came as a replacement for Nigeria's Universal Primary Education scheme of the 6-3-3-4 system of primary education. The 9-3-4 system of education was designed in conformity with the MDGs and Education For All, EFA. The UBE involves 6 years of Primary School education and 3 years of Junior Secondary School education, culminating in 9 years of uninterrupted schooling, and transition from one class to another is automatic but determined through continuous assessment.

Secondary Education

Students spend six years in Secondary School, that is 3 years of JSS (Junior Secondary School), and 3 years of SSS (Senior Secondary School). By Senior Secondary School Class 2 (SS2), students are taking the GCE O'Levels exam, which is not mandatory, but most students take it to prepare for the Senior Secondary Certificate Examination. The Senior Secondary School Exam is taken in the last year of secondary school (SS3). Private organizations, the State government or the Federal government manage secondary schools in Nigeria.

Promotional Examinations

With the introduction of 9-3-4 system of education in Nigeria, the recipient of the education would spend six years in primary school, three years in junior secondary school, three years in senior secondary school, and four years in tertiary institution. The six years spent in primary school and the three years spent in junior secondary school are merged to form the nine in the 9-3-4 system. Altogether, the students must spend a minimum period of six years in Secondary School. During this period, students are expected to spend three years in Junior Secondary School and three years in Senior Secondary School.

UGANDA

Comparing to other countries in East Africa, Uganda's education system has the most rigorous academic and scholastic standards. Recently, due to the liberalization of the education sector along with Uganda's rapid economic growth, there has been an astronomical increase in the number of private schools in Uganda. Consequently, Uganda has seen an influx of people seeking to study in Uganda. The largest influx of students has come from East Africa, particularly; Kenya, Tanzania, Rwanda, Burundi, Sudan, and Congo.

The system of education in Uganda has a structure of 7 years of primary education, 6 years of secondary education (divided into 4 years of lower secondary and 2 years of upper secondary school), and 3 to 5 years of post secondary education.

Primary Education

In 1999 there were 6 million pupils receiving primary education, compared to only 2 million in 1986. Numbers received a boost in 1997 when free primary education was made available for four children per family. Only some of primary school graduates go on to take any form of secondary education. This is contingent upon them passing their Primary Leaving Examinations (PLE).

Secondary Education

Lower secondary consists of 4 years of schooling at the end of which students Ordinary-level exams (O-level) in at least 8 subjects. Upper secondary consists of 2 years of schooling at the end of which students sit Advanced-level exams (A-level) in at least 3 subjects.

The curriculum for lower secondary is currently being reviewed by the National Curriculum Development Centre, and a new curriculum is expected to be rolled out in 2014 or 2015.

Three-year technical schools provide an alternative to lower secondary school. Alternatives for graduates from lower secondary school include: 2-3 year Technical institutes; 2 year Primary Teacher Colleges (PTC); Department Training Colleges (DTCs) and Upper secondary schools

MALAWI

The government of Malawi recognises the importance of pre-school education, and encourages communities to set up their own pre-schools, but does not support pre-schools financially. With no funds to support pre-schools, most of them are run on a voluntary basis and are unregistered. Most teachers work for free, and have no resources to help them teach, lacking the very basics including blackboards and chalk, let alone books and toys which might commonly be associated with pre-school education in the West.

It is rare that pre-schools have their own school buildings, and many pre-schools share facilities with local churches or other buildings built for a different purpose. Not all children have access to pre-school education as access is dependent upon location and upon voluntary community involvement. Official data on the number of pre-schools in Malawi is difficult to find because schools are unregistered.

Primary Education

Primary school education in Malawi is provided by the government, and is free to all students in Malawi. Free primary school education was introduced to Malawi in 1994, and in the first year after the policy change, primary school enrolment in Malawi tripled from 1.6 million students, to over 3 million students. However, while primary school enrolment increased, there was a national shortage of classrooms and qualified teachers to deal with the huge increase in students. Although more students now have access to education in Malawi, the quality of education has decreased. Today, most primary schools in Malawi are under-resourced, under-staffed, and under-funded, creating extremely challenging teaching and learning conditions for teachers and students alike.

Primary school education in Malawi is made up of eight years, Standard 1 to Standard 8. Although the official primary school age group in Malawi is categorised as 6-13, it is very common for students of varying ages to attend primary school, as many students have to repeat some primary years. Primary school students in Malawi learn a variety of subjects, and take examinations in English, ChiChewa, Mathematics, science, and social studies. Students must gain a Primary School Leaving Certificate based on their Standard 8 final exam results in order to progress to secondary school.

Most primary schools in Malawi are very basic, lacking the most fundamental resources, including textbooks and basic teaching materials. Although many primary schools have brick classroom blocks, many students learn outside in temporary structures, making teaching impossible during the rainy season.

The shortage of teachers in Malawi is due to two main reasons. Firstly, there are not enough trained teachers who have completed all their necessary qualifications to go around, and, secondly, primary schools in Malawi must provide teachers' houses to attract good teachers to their school. Teachers' houses can be very expensive to build but, without them, it is impossible to attract new teachers to the area.

Although primary education in Malawi is free, students are required to purchase their own school uniform, pens, and notebooks, which many families find difficult. Rates for drop-outs are high, and, according to UNESCO, only 58 per cent of children will complete a full course of primary school, and 20 per cent of children repeat one or more school years, often several times, if they have had to take significant time out of school and have fallen behind. It is very common for children in Malawi to come in and out of school depending on their family situation, employment responsibilities, pregnancy and marriage at a young age, sickness, and more. By the time students leave primary school, many of them are far older than primary age, having repeated several years, and many lose interest and drop out all together.

For most people in Malawi, primary education is the highest level of education they will achieve. As a result, primary education is an essential aspect of community life in Malawi, and is critical to the development of Malawi as a whole. Many of the basic skills and foundational knowledge required for life must be learned in these formative years. Therefore, it is critical to Malawi's development to support primary education.

Secondary Education

Secondary school education in Malawi is provided by the government as well as privately, but is not free to students who must pay school fees. Fees, even at the lower amount, pose a huge burden to families in Malawi who struggle to raise enough money to send their children to secondary school at these rates. Secondary schools in Malawi are run in four years

Although many secondary schools are better resourced than their primary school counterparts, secondary school education in Malawi still varies greatly and is extremely under-resourced. Secondary school students in Malawi still struggle with poor student to teacher ratios, access to books and learning materials, adequate classroom facilities, and adequately trained teachers.

Although secondary school education remains a basic public service in many countries across the world, for most people in Malawi, the chance to attend secondary school is something very special, and millions of children in Malawi will never get the chance to experience secondary education at all. For those who do attend, inadequate teachers and a lack of proper facilities will still prove a challenge to their education. By the time the few students who will attend secondary school get to the end of their schooling, only the smallest fraction will ever go on to university. Secondary school education in Malawi remains something of great importance to most Malawians, and a goal which most young people strive towards.

REFERENCES

Algeria country profile. (May 2008) *Library of Congress Federal Research Division* .

Aliu, S, (2001). "The Competitive Drive, New Technologies and Employment: The Human Capital Link". A Paper presented at the Second Tripartite Conference of Manpower Planners. Chelsea Hotel, Abuja.

Bird, K. and Higgins, K. (2009) *Conflict, education and the intergenerational transmission of poverty in Northern Uganda.* London: Overseas Development Institute.

Celine, F. (2009). *Age at First Child: Does Education Delay Fertility Timing? The Case of Kenya.* Policy Research Working Paper. World Bank.

Education in Ethiopia (Ethiopian Embassy website)

Eshiwani, G.S. (1990). *Implementing Educational Policies in Kenya.* Africa Technical Department Series Discussion Paper. World Bank.

Martha, N. (2003) "Women's Education: A Global Challenge" *Sign: Journal of Women in Culture and Society,* 2003, Vol. 29, No. 2.

Ministry of Education. 2007. National strategic plan for education in Egypt: towards a paradigm shift 2007/08-2011/12. Cairo: MoE

Pankhurst, R. (1972) *"Education in Ethiopia during the Italian Fascist Occupation (1936-1941)", International Journal of African Historical Studies,* 5 (1972), p. 371

Schultz, T.P. (2002). "Why Governments should Invest More to Educate Girls, *World Development,* Vol. 30, No. 2, pp. 207-225.

UNESCO Institute of Statistics, 2008

World Bank (2007). "Improving Quality, Equality, and Efficiency in the Education Sector: Fostering a Competent Generation of Youth." Education Sector Policy Note. Footnote 6, p. 5. The World Bank, Washington, DC".

6

Elementary Education in Australia

AUSTRALIA

Education in Australia is compulsory between the ages of five and fifteen to seventeen, depending on the state or territory, and date of birth. Post-compulsory education is regulated within the Australian Qualifications Framework, a unified system of national qualifications in schools, vocational education and training and the higher education sector.

Education in Australia is primarily the responsibility of the states and territories. Each state or territory government provides funding and regulates the public and private schools within its governing area. The federal government helps fund the public universities, but was not involved in setting curriculum. As of 2012, the Australian National Curriculum, under development and trial for several years, has already been adopted by some schools and will become mandatory soon. Generally, education in Australia follows the three-tier model which includes primary education, followed by secondary education and tertiary education.

The Programme for International Student Assessment (PISA) 2006 evaluation ranked the Australian education system as sixth for reading, eighth for science and thirteenth for mathematics, on a worldwide scale including 56 countries. The PISA 2010 evaluation ranked the Australian education system as sixth for reading, seventh for science and ninth for mathematics, an improvement relative to the 2006 rankings.

The Education index published with the United Nation's Human Development Index in 2008, based on data from 2006, lists

Australia as 0.993, amongst the highest in the world, tied for first with Denmark and Finland

Pre-school

Pre-school and pre-prep programmes in Australia is relatively unregulated, and is not compulsory. The first exposure many Australian children have to learn with others outside of traditional parenting is day care or a parent-run playgroup. This sort of activity is not generally considered schooling, as pre-school education is separate from primary school in all states and territories, except Western Australia where pre-school education is taught as part of the primary school system. In Queensland, pre-school programmes are often called Kindergarten or Pre-Prep, and are usually privately run but attract state government funding if run for at least 600 hours a year and delivered by a registered teacher.

Pre-school is offered to three- to five-year-olds; attendance numbers vary widely between the states, but 85.7 per cent of children attended pre-school the year before school. The year before a child is due to attend primary school is the main year for pre-school education. This year is far more commonly attended, and may take the form of a few hours of activity during weekdays.

Responsibility for pre-schools in New South Wales and Victoria, lies with the Department of Community Services and the Department of Education and Early Childhood Development (DEECD), respectively. In all other states and territories of Australia, responsibility for pre-schools lie with the relevant education department.

School Education

As mentioned earlier, school education in Australia is compulsory between certain ages as specified by state or territory legislation. Depending on the state or territory, and date of birth of the child, school is compulsory from the age of five to six to the age of fifteen to seventeen. In recent years, over three quarters of students stay at school until they are seventeen.

Government schools (also known as public schools) are free to attend for Australian citizens and permanent residents, while Catholic and independent schools usually charge attendance fees. However in addition to attendance fees; stationery, textbooks, uniforms, school camps and other schooling costs are not covered under government funding. Regardless of whether a school is part of the Government, Catholic or independent systems, they are required to adhere to the same curriculum frameworks of their state or territory. Most school students wear uniforms, although there are varying expectations and some Australian schools do not require uniforms.

Catholic and Independent Schools

In 2010 66 per cent of students in Australia attended government schools, 20 per cent attended Catholic schools and 14 per cent attended independent schools. In 2000 these figures were 69, 20 per cent and 11 per cent respectively.

Most Catholic schools are either run by their local parish, local diocese and their state's Catholic education department independent schools include schools operated by secular educational philosophies such as Montessori, however, the majority of independent schools are religious, being Protestant, Jewish, Islamic or non-denominational. Some Catholic and independent schools charge high fees, because of this Government funding for these schools often comes under criticism.

NEW ZEALAND

Education in New Zealand follows the three-tier model which includes primary schools, followed by secondary schools (high schools) and tertiary education at universities and/or polytechnics.

The Education Index published with the UN's Human Development Index in 2008, based on data from 2006, lists New Zealand as 0.993, amongst the highest in the world, tied for first with Denmark, Finland and Australia. Also, for 2011, the Education Index showed that New Zealand was the first, with 1.000, the highest.

Primary and Secondary Education

Education is free and compulsory between the ages of 6 and 16, although in very special cases an exemption can be gained after applying to the Ministry Of Education (MOE). These may be granted to students who are close to 16, have been experiencing some ongoing difficulty at school, and have a job already lined up. Families wishing to home educate their children can apply for exemption. To get an exemption from enrollment at a registered school, they must satisfy the Secretary of Education that their child will be taught "as regularly and as well as in a registered school".

Children almost always start school on their 5th birthday, or the first School Day after it. Many children attend some form of early childhood education before they begin school such as:

- Play Centre (birth to school age)
- Kindergarten (ages 3–5)
- Kohanga Reo
- Licensed Early Childhood Centres (ages 0–5)
- Chartered Early Childhood Centres (ages 0–5)

Free primary and secondary education is a right for all New Zealand citizens and permanent residents from a student's fifth birthday until the end of the calendar year following the student's 19th birthday, and is compulsory for students between the ages of 6 and 16 (15 with parental and school permission). A recent proposal by the New Zealand Government, called School Plus, would see students required to remain in some form of education until age 18. Disabled students with special educational needs can stay until the end of the calendar year they turn 21.

Most students start when they turn 5, and remain in school for the full 13 years. Students living more than 5 kilometres walking distance from the nearest school (or public transport to school) may be exempted from attending school but may be required to enroll in a correspondence school. Many schools contract public transport operators to provide school buses that deliver students to the school gate in the morning and home again at the end of the school day.

Between 2000 and 2007, most New Zealand schools moved towards designating school class levels based on the years of schooling of the student cohort. The introduction of NCEA in the early 2000s, computerised enrolment and school roll return guideline changes, amongst others, have been drivers for this change. Before this, a system of Forms, Standards and Juniors or

Primers was used. Although those older terms are no longer used for most school administration they still appear in education legislation, at some schools, and in talk with older generations, who often prefer to use the terms they are more familiar with.

There are 13 academic year levels, numbered 1 through to 13. Under the old system of Forms, Standards and Juniors, there were two Junior years followed by four Standard years in primary school, followed by seven Forms. Forms 1 and 2 were in intermediate school and the remaining five were in secondary school.

Types of Schools by Years

While there is overlap in some schools, primary school ends at Year 8 and secondary school at Year 13. The last two years of primary school are frequently taken at a separate intermediate school instead of a primary school, leaving 'contributing' primary schools to end at Year 6. Some areas though have 'full' primary schools which go to year 8. Outside of the following categories, many private schools, state area schools and state integrated schools take students from Years 0 to 13, or Years 7 to 13.

Categories of schools are the following:

- *Contributing Primary School:* Years 1–6 (ages 5–11). There are no private contributing primaries.
- *Full Primary School*: Years 1–8 (ages 5–13). Common among integrated and private schools.
- *Intermediate School*: Years 7–8 (ages 10–13). Only two non-state intermediate schools exist.
- *Secondary School*: Years 9–13 (ages 12–18)

There are three types of schools: state, private (or registered or independent) and state integrated schools as per the classification on funding. State and state integrated schools are government funded. Private schools receive about 25 per cent of their funding from the government, and rely on tuition fees for the rest. State integrated schools are former private schools which are now "integrated" into the state system under the Private Schools.

While the state covers tuition for New Zealand citizens and permanent residents, students must still pay for course materials and related costs. Also, almost all schools charge a tax deductible "donation" that most parents pay. Private or independent schools charge tuition fees while state integrated schools may charge an additional levy ("attendance dues") for the upkeep of school buildings. International students holding valid student visas can also be enrolled in state funded schools, provided they pay the appropriate international student tuition fees. Because Australian citizens and permanent residents do not require visas to study in New Zealand, they are classed as domestic students and therefore do not pay international fees. A number of schools use international student fees to supplement their state funding.

REFERENCES

csi.gsb.stanford.edu/podcast
www.impeloverseas.com › *Study abroad* › *AUSTRALIA*
www.studyinaustralia.gov.au › *Home* › *Courses* › *Schools*
www.newzealandeducated.com/
en.wikipedia.org/wiki/Education_ in_ New _Zealand
www.newzealandeducation.com/primary.html
newzealand.angloinfo.com › ... › *Schooling & Education*

7

Elementary Education in Latin America

Elementary education in Latin American countries are discussed by taking Argentina and Brazil as examples.

ARGENTINA

Education in Argentina is a responsibility shared by the national government, the provinces and federal district and private institutions, though basic guidelines have historically been set by the Ministry of Education. Education at all levels, including universities, have always been free and not requiring to pay any kind of fee.

Primary Education

Education in Argentina at the primary level is complimentary and obligatory for the inhabitants. Different laws set forth the quality and standards of education in elementary levels. The schools follow the teaching methods of induction, deduction, analysis, synthesis, interrogation, and demonstration. At the completion of the schools, a diploma called "Certificado de Terminacion de Estudios Primarios" is awarded to the students, allowing them to peruse higher education. Primary education comprises the grades 1–6. Because of the system that was in place until 1995 i.e., 7 years of primary school plus 5 or 6 of secondary school, primary schools used to offer grades 1–7, although most are already converted to accept 8th and 9th, others chose to eliminate 7th grade altogether, forcing the students to complete the next cycle in another institution.

Secondary Education

Secondary education in Argentina, better known as "Polimodal" permits the students to choose individual orientations. Secondary education in Argentina is called *Polimodal* i.e., having multiple modes, since it allows the student to choose his/her orientation. Polimodal is obligatory and its completion is a requirement to enter colleges across the nation. This level is not compulsory for the students, but a successful completion of the secondary studies results in admission at the college levels to continue further education.

Polimodal is usually 3 years of schooling, although some schools have a fourth year.

Conversely to what happened on primary schools, most secondary schools in Argentina contained grades 8th and 9th, plus Polimodal (old secondary) but then started converting to accept also 7th grade students.

This is different however, in the city of Buenos Aires (and several provinces), where Polimodal does not exist. The capital keeps in use the Traditional Argentine education system, composed of seven years of primary education and five years of secondary education (the first three of which are of a more general education, with more focus on the specialization starting in the last two years).

The secondary education system is thus divided in three large groups, "Bachiller" schools (very similar to grammar schools with a huge emphasis on humanistic studies), "Comercial" schools (focusing on economic sciences and everything related to it) and "Escuelas Técnicas" (with a focus on technical and scientific assignments, this one having the particularity of lasting six years instead of five, it used to be called "Industrial") each one subdivided in more specific orientations related to its main branch. Currently there are no plans to adopt the Polimodal system in the city of Buenos Aires, but rather, several provinces with that system are seriously considering a reform of it, with many opting for the traditional system still used in Buenos Aires.

In December 2006 Argentine Congress approved a new National Education Law restoring the old system of primary followed by secondary education, making secondary education obligatory and a right, and increasing the length of compulsory education to 13 years

Education in Argentina has made the country one of the most literate lands in Latin America. The system of education existing in Argentina imparts knowledge not only to the native inhabitants but to the alien population too, leading in extensive spread of basic schooling among the assorted residents of the land.

BRAZIL

Until the 20th century, Brazil was a large rural nation with low social and economic standards comparing to the average North American and European realities at the time and it achieved independence in 1822. Its economy was based on the primary sector, possessing an unskilled and increasingly larger workforce, composed by both free people (including slave owners) and slaves or their direct descendants.

With the massive post-war expansion that lasts to date, the government focused on strengthening Brazil's tertiary education, while simultaneously neglecting assistance to primary and secondary education. The problems of primary and secondary education were compounded by significant quality differences across regions with the Northeast suffering dramatically.

Today, Brazil struggles to improve the public education offered at earlier stages and maintain the high standards that the population has come to expect from public universities. The choice on public funding is an issue.

Education in Brazil is regulated by the Federal Government through the Ministry of Education, which defines the guiding principles for the organization of education programmes. Local governments are responsible for establishing state and education programmes following the guidelines and using the funding supplied by the federal government.

In a period of history when the world had a largely illiterate population, the Portuguese Empire, was home to one of the first universities founded in Europe — the University of Coimbra, which is still one of the oldest universities in continuous operation. Throughout the centuries of Portuguese rule, Brazilian students, mostly graduated in the Jesuit missions and seminaries, were allowed and even encouraged to enroll at higher education in mainland Portugal.

Organization and Structure

Education is divided into three levels, with several grades in each level. Fundamental education (the first education level, including fundamental education I and II) is free for everyone (including adults), and mandatory for children between the ages of 6-14. Middle education (the second education level) is also free, but it is not mandatory. Higher education (including graduate degrees) is free at public universities.

Pre-school Education

Pre-school education is entirely optional, and exists to aid in the development of children under 6 years. It aims to assist in all areas of child development, including motor skills, cognitive skills, and social skills while providing fertile ground for the later acquisition of knowledge and learning. There are day nurseries for children under 2 years, kindergartens for 2-3 year olds, and preschools for children 4 and up. Public pre-schools are provided by city government.

Elementary School

Fundamental Education is mandatory for children ages 6–14. There are 9 "years". The current "First Year" broadly corresponds to the former Pre-School last year of private institutions, and its aim is to achieve literacy. Generally speaking, the only prerequisite for enrolling in first year is that a child should be 6 years old, but some education systems allow children younger than 6 to enroll in first year (as long as they turn 6 during the first academic semester). Older students who, for whatever reason have not completed their fundamental education are allowed to attend, though those over 18 are separated from the younger children.

Fundamental Education is divided in two stages, called *Ensino Fundamental I* (years 1-5) and *Ensino Fundamental II* (years 6-9). During *Ensino Fundamental I* each group of students is usually assisted by a single teacher. As for *Ensino Fundamental II*, there are as many teachers as subjects.

The length of the school year is set by the National Education Bases and Guidelines Law at at least 200 days. Fundamental schools must provide students with at least 800 hours of activities per year. The actual school calendar is set by individual schools which, in rural areas, often organize their calendars according to planting and harvesting seasons. Public fundamental schools are funded by municipal and state governments. The education is similar to the British.

Secondary School

Secondary Education takes 3 years. The minimum is 2,200 hours of coursework over 3 years. Students must have finished their Fundamental education before they are allowed to enroll in Ensino Médio. Secondary education core curriculum comprises Portuguese (including Portuguese language, Brazilian and Portuguese literature), foreign language (usually English also Spanish and very rarely French today), History, Geography, Mathematics, Physics, Chemistry and Biology. Recently Philosophy and Sociology, which were banned during the military dictatorship (1964–1985), became compulsory again.

The Brazilian education level is considered low compared to developed countries, especially in public schools, despite its being low in many of their private counterparts.

REFERENCES

Harbison, R. and *Hanushek*, E. (1992), *Educational performance of the poor: lessons from rural northeast Brazil* New York: Oxford University Press.

8

Elementary Education in North America

Elementary education in the United States, Canada and Mexico are detailed in the section.

UNITED STATES

The rapid changes in cognitive, social, and moral growth of an elementary school student makes the elementary classroom an ideal setting for shaping individual attitudes and behaviors. The elementary classroom may provide the best opportunity to set in place moral and ethical characteristics and understandings that have the potential to improve society. Children in the elementary schools are still malleable, and this emphasis on character education is seen as a particularly urgent matter in American classrooms. In fact, the socialization of children in America is no longer viewed as the sole responsibility of their parents.

The view of using the elementary classroom as a stage for molding future citizens of a democratic society is not new, but it does give rise to controversy regarding programmes and methods, as parents may disagree with specific curriculum being promoted by local, state, or national agencies. For example, sex education at the elementary school level has been the object of much debate among religious and special interest groups.

Unlike many other nations, the United States does not have a national curriculum. As mentioned previously, control of the schools is reserved to the states, which in turn give local school districts some control over what is taught and how it is taught. Curriculum may be looked at as a negotiated set of beliefs about what students should know or be able to do. Until recently, states and local districts had significant latitude in the development of elementary curriculum.

Formal education for women started with the American Revolution, and for black children with the American Civil War However, homeschooling remained predominant, especially in the south, until the mid-19th century.

Government supported, free public schools for all started being established after the revolution, and expanded in the 19th century. By 1870, all states had free elementary schools, albeit only in urban centers. As the 20th century drew nearer, states started passing laws to make schooling compulsory, and by 1910, 72 per cent of children attended school. Private schools continued to spread during this time, as well as colleges and—in the rural centers—land grant colleges. The year of 1910 also saw the first true high schools. During the rest of the 20th century, educational efforts centered on reducing the inequality of the schooling system.

In the U.S.A. there is not a national system of education; it is mainly the responsibility of the individual states. Although the Federal Government often gives money to schools, it exercises very little control over administration or curriculum. Each of 50 states has its own school system and every state wants young people to go to school. The age limits vary 7 to 16 or 6 to 18. Every child gets minimum 13 years of education regardless to child's race, religion, sex, learning problems, physical handicap or ability to speak English. Education is different in various areas of the U.S.A. and there are usually grades 1-12.

All schools are controlled by an elected local body known as the "school board" and by the city and state in which the school is located. Therefore there is quite a large difference between schools in different cities and states. The majority of all schools are public schools, i.e. publicly owned schools, financed by state or local governments. These schools are free. (Public schools in the USA never mean private schools as they do in England). Then there are also private schools which charge high tuition fees and this is why usually only children from rich families attend these schools. But nearly all private schools offer scholarships. Only those private schools which are financed by various religious groups or organizations are, however, much cheaper.

All public schools are mixed schools (co-educational), some private or church schools remain single-sex. School attendance is compulsory in the United States between 6 and 16 and the system of education is divided into pre-school and elementary, secondary and higher education.

After each term or quarter children get a report-card which informs their parents about their results at school, and at the end of the school year they get a transcript. Marks in most US schools are:

A (excellent)
B (superior, above average)
C (satisfactory)
D (passing grade)
E (completely unsatisfactory).

Pre-school and Elementary Education

Pre-school and elementary education includes nursery schools and kindergartens which are for children at the age of 4-6. Most of them are private. Many public schools have kindergartens attached, for the age group between 5 and 6. These kindergartens do not charge any money.

Compulsory education starts at the age of 6. Both elementary and secondary education is comprehensive in the U.S.A.—it means that there is no selection for various types of schools (every school learns the same subjects). Years are called "Grades" in the U.S.A. Elementary school lasts between 6 and 11 years of age. It is from the first till the fifth grade. The children at elementary schools learn to read, write, and do arithmetic, elementary science, history, geography, arts and crafts, physical education and music. The atmosphere at elementary schools is usually friendly. Teachers keep to the idea that children's happiness and interest are the two most important things.

Secondary Education

Secondary education is based on the ideal of mass education with equal opportunity for all.

Over 90 per cent of students continue in school until the age of 18. Secondary education is provided by Middle Schools (from 11 to 14 years of age—sixth, seventh and eighth grade) in the areas where they exist, or by High Schools which are often divided into Junior High School (at the age 11 to 14 -Sixth to eighth grade) and Senior High School (at the age of 15 to 18—ninth, tenth, eleventh and twelfth grade). Where the population is very big, Junior and Senior High schools can be separate institutions.

In large towns or communities there may be a wide choice of secondary schools. In some places you may have the opportunity to attend a specialized school, such as a school for science, a school for the performing arts or a high school for the navy, or to go to the central high school in the area. If a student chooses to remain at the central high school, he or she, again, may have an opportunity to choose among a variety of subjects from traditional ones such as English, modern languages, mathematics, science, history, geography, civics, physical education and from many elective subjects (European history, world political issues, Business education, Foreign languages, Music, Driver education, Health, Computer skills, home management, Black history etc.).

High schools generally organize much activity outside the classroom; many of them have football, basketball and baseball teams, an orchestra, a choir or a jazz band, and various clubs and societies. High schools in the USA are comprehensive, coeducational secondary schools. Some high schools may offer specialized courses or subjects, such as business, computer science, running a shop, or music and film appreciation.

Education in the United States is mainly provided by the public sector, with control and funding coming from three levels: local, state, and federal, in that order. Child education is compulsory. There are also a large number and wide variety of higher education institutions throughout the country that one can choose to attend, both publicly and privately administered.

Public education is universally available. School curricula, funding, teaching, employment, and other policies are set through locally elected school boards with jurisdiction over school districts with many directives from state legislatures. School districts are usually separate from other local jurisdictions, with independent officials and budgets. Educational standards and standardized testing decisions are usually made by state governments.

Basic Curricular Structure

Generally, at the high school level, students take a broad variety of classes without special emphasis in any particular subject. Students are required to take a certain minimum number of mandatory subjects, but may choose additional subjects (electives) to fill out their required hours of learning.

The following minimum courses of study in mandatory subjects are required in nearly all U.S. high schools:

- Science (usually three years minimum, normally biology, chemistry and physics)
- Mathematics (usually four years minimum, normally including algebra, geometry, pre-calculus, statistics, and even calculus)
- English (usually four years minimum, including literature, humanities, composition, oral languages, etc.)
- Social sciences (usually three years minimum, including various history, government/economics courses)
- Physical education (at least two years)

Many states require a "health" course in which students learn about anatomy, nutrition, first aid, sexuality, drug awareness and birth control. Anti-drug use programmes are also usually part of health courses. In many cases, however, options are provided for students to "test out" of this requirement or complete independent study to meet it. Foreign language and some form of art education are also a mandatory part of the curriculum in some schools.

Home Schooling

Many select moral or religious reasons for homeschooling their children. The second main category is "unschooling," those who prefer a non-standard approach to education.

Most homeschooling advocates are wary of the established educational institutions for various reasons. Some are religious conservatives who see nonreligious education as contrary to their moral or religious systems, or who wish to add religious instruction to the educational curriculum (and who may be unable to afford a church-operated private school or where the only available school may teach views contrary to those of the parents). Others feel that they can more effectively tailor a curriculum to suit an individual student's academic strengths and weaknesses, especially those with singular needs or disabilities. Still others feel that the negative social pressures of schools (such as bullying, drugs, crime, sex, and other school-related problems) are detrimental to a child's proper development. Parents often form groups to help each other in the homeschooling process, and may even assign classes to different parents, similar to public and private schools.

Opposition to homeschooling comes from varied sources, including teachers' organizations and school districts. The National Education Association the largest labor union in the United States, has been particularly vocal in the past. Opponents' stated concerns fall into several broad categories, including fears of poor academic quality, and lack of socialization with others. At this time, over half of states have oversight into monitoring or measuring the academic progress of home schooled students, with all but ten requiring some form of notification to the state.

Public and Private Schools

In the United States, state and local government have primary responsibility for education. The Federal Department of Education plays a role in standards setting and education finance, and some primary and secondary schools, for the children of military employees, are run by the Department of Defense.

Public school systems are supported by a combination of local, state, and federal government funding. Because a large portion of school revenues come from local property taxes, public schools vary widely in the resources they have available per student. Class size also varies from one district to another. Curriculum decisions in public schools are made largely at the local and state levels; the federal government has limited influence. In most districts, a locally elected school board runs schools. The school board appoints an official called the superintendent of schools to manage the schools in the district.

Admission to individual public schools is usually based on residency. To compensate for differences in school quality based on geography, school systems serving large cities and portions of large cities often have "magnet schools" that provide enrollment to a specified number of non-resident students in addition to serving all resident students. This special enrollment is usually decided by lottery with equal numbers of males and females chosen.

Private schools in the United States include parochial schools (affiliated with religious denominations), non-profit independent schools, and for-profit private schools. Private schools charge varying rates depending on geographic location, the school's expenses, and the availability of funding from sources, other than tuition.

Private schools offer the advantages of smaller classes, under twenty students in a typical elementary classroom, for example; a higher teacher/student ratio across the school day, greater individualized attention and in the more competitive schools, expert college placement services. Unless specifically designed to do so, private schools usually cannot offer the services required by students with serious or multiple learning, emotional, or behavioral issues.

CANADA

Education in Canada is for the most part provided publicly, funded and overseen by federal, provincial, and local governments. Education is within provincial jurisdiction and the curriculum is overseen by the province. Education in Canada is generally divided into primary education, followed by secondary education and post-secondary.

Education in both English and French has been available in most places across Canada, although French Second Language education/French Immersion is available to anglophone students across Canada. According to an announcement of Canadian Minister of Citizenship and Immigration, Canada is introducing a new, fast-track system to let foreign students and graduates with Canadian work experience become permanent eligible residents in Canada.

Within the provinces under the ministry of education, there are district school boards administering the educational programmes. Education is compulsory up to the age of 16 in every province in Canada, except for Manitoba, Ontario and New

Brunswick, where the compulsory age is 18, or as soon as a high school diploma has been achieved. In some provinces early leaving exemptions can be granted under certain circumstances at 14.

Elementary, secondary, and post-secondary education in Canada is a provincial responsibility and there are many variations between the provinces. Some educational fields are supported at various levels by federal departments. The Department of Indian and Northern Affairs Canada is responsible for the education of First Nations. Vocational training can be subsidized by the Learning branch of Human Resources and Skills Development Canada (a federal department).

Junior Kindergarten (or equivalent), as an official programme, exists only in Ontario currently. Kindergarten (or its equivalent) is available in every province, but provincial funding, and the number of hours provided varies widely. Starting at grade one, at age six or seven, there is universal publicly funded access up to grade twelve (or equivalent). Dependent on the province the age of mandatory entry is at 4–7 years. Children are required to attend school until the age of sixteen (eighteen in Ontario and New Brunswick). In many places, publicly funded high school courses are offered to the adult population. The ratio of high school graduates versus non diploma-holders is changing rapidly, partly due to changes in the labour market that require people to have a high school diploma and, in many cases, a university degree.

Private Schools

About 5.6 per cent of students are in private schools. A minority of these are elite private schools, which are attended by only a small fraction of students, but do have a great deal of prestige and prominence. It is not unusual for the wealthy and prominent in Canada to send their children to public schools, especially in the lower grades. A far larger portion of private schools are religious based institutions.

Private schools have historically been less common on the Canadian Prairies and were often forbidden under municipal and provincial statutes enacted to provide equality of education to students regardless of family income.

MEXICO

Education in Mexico is regulated by the Secretariat of Public Education. Education standards are set by this Ministry at all levels except in "autonomous" universities chartered by the government. Accreditation of private schools is accomplished by a mandatory approval and registration with this institution.

In Mexico, basic education is normally divided in three steps: primary school (primaria), comprising grades 1-6; Junior high School (secundaria), comprising grades 7-9; and High School (preparatoria), comprising grades 10-12.

1917 Constitution provides that education should avoid privileges of religion, and that one religion or its members may not be given preference in education over another. Religious instruction is prohibited in public schools; however, religious associations are free to maintain private schools, which receive no public funds. Proof of Mexican citizenship is required to attend public schools for free, but foreigners can attend public schools by paying a tuition.

In the same fashion to other education systems, education may be described in identifiable stages, such as Primary School, Junior High School, High School, Higher education, and Postgraduate education.

Primary School

The terms "Primary School" or "Elementary School" usually corresponds to *primaria,* comprising grades 1-6, when the student's age is 6 to 12 years old. It starts the basic compulsory education system.

Depending on the school, a bilingual education may be offered from the beginning, where half the day instruction is in Spanish, and the rest is in a second language, for example, English or French.

In Spanish, the general term for "school" is escuela, but in Mexico, it is common to use escuela for state-owned schools, which are the majority, while the term colegio (cognate with "college") is reserved for private schools, usually charging higher tuition fees.

Junior High School

The terms "Junior High School" or "Middle School" usually